novum **pro**

D1740828

Lighting the Candle

"Expressing the Need for Solidarity Behind
Invigorating & Revising the Great Game of Rugby Union"

by

COLIN SIMMONDS
with
IAIN RUSSELL
and special support from

SIMMERGY

SIMMERGY Ltd.

novum pro

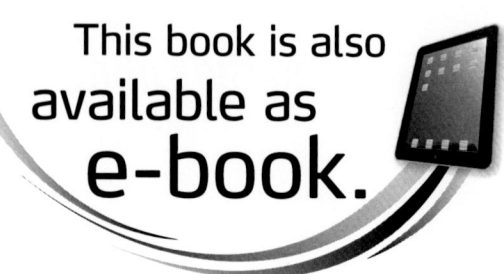

This book is also
available as
e-book.

www.novum-publishing.co.uk

SPECIAL ACKNOWLEDGEMENT

Colin Simmonds and SIMMERGY Ltd. wish to acknowledge the tremendous contribution to the writing of this Book by IAIN RUSSELL.

Iain is both an accomplished rugby coach and businessman, having worked with Glasgow, Northampton Saints and Scottish junior representative fifteens, as well as driving the financial and general management affairs of several companies, both large and small.

Without Iain's patience, his attention to detail and insight, this book would not have been possible.

My sincere thanks and appreciation go to him.

Colin Simmonds
Bath, May 2019

Contents

THE STRUCTURE OF THE BOOK

THE GAME AS IT IS TODAY

INTRODUCTION

Setting the scene, creating the right tone and nature of the Book. Explanation of the design criteria; the overall intention and pinpointing the accountability and responsibilities of players, adjudicators, legislators, coaches, teachers and parents

Chapter 2

FOUNDATION POSITIONS & POSITIONING

The Essential Foundation of the Book

Describing in literal and philosophical terms just what is expected of a player in each position. Plus what is expected of the referee and assistant referees.

Includes Player Skills
- ✔ Team & Individual
- ✔ Use of width – lateral running
- ✔ In search of Space
- ✔ Playing what's in front of you

Adjudicator Skills
- ✔ Enforce the Laws, with...
- ✔ Sympathetic interpretation

THE PLATFORM FOR THE FUTURE

Chapter 3
ENFORCEMENT

Listing the areas of controversy. The areas of the game that are suffering with law interpretations and unsympathetic enforcement. Describing the irritants for players and, perhaps most importantly, for spectators. Provide the message to the legislators: 'stop fiddling and enforce the laws as they are!'

Chapter 4,5,6

OLD & NEW AND ALWAYS VITAL, ASPECTS OF THE GAME

Application of Skill - specifically in terms of:
- ✔ General Defending
- ✔ Attacking – from scrum, line out and broken play

Utilisation of Possession
- ✔ Peripheral Vision
- ✔ Support Play
- ✔ Kicking & chasing
- ✔ The breakdown
- ✔ Using space and winning 'overlaps'.
- ✔ Contact

THE ONLY WAY FORWARD

CHAPTERS 8, 9, 10

THE SKILLS, AIMS & RESPONSIBILITIES OF PLAYERS, COACHES AND SPECTATORS

Positive Thinking; the perils for Children in the game
Lessons for Coaches and Teachers
- ✔ Setting the Standard
- ✔ The 'human qualities', plus knowledge and experience required
- ✔ Living with 'Acceptable Mediocrity'
- ✔ Avoiding 'bish-bosh-collision' rugby
- ✔ Where to now?

Chapters 11 & 12

IN SEARCH OF EXCELLENCE & THE FUTURE

- • Seeking Excellence from whatever level!
- • What does it all mean? Where do we go now?
- • What IS the future of this great Game?

There are a number of diagrams plus commentary contained within this book that enables the reader to visualise what is being said in the narrative.

THE LEGEND FOR ALL DIAGRAMS:

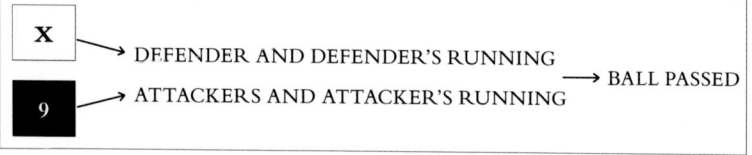

X ⟶ DEFENDER AND DEFENDER'S RUNNING

⟶ BALL PASSED

9 ⟶ ATTACKERS AND ATTACKER'S RUNNING

CHAPTER ONE

WHY THIS BOOK? AN INTRODUCTION

*'The first step to getting anywhere
is deciding you're not willing
to stay where you are.'*
(Anonymous)

*'Life has no meaning except in
terms of responsibility.'*
(Reinhold Niebuhr)

There are many 'books on rugby' so what is the purpose of this one?

Why should you pick this up and while away a few PRECIOUS hours reading it?

This book is not a coaching manual, although it does provide hints and guidance that are aimed at pointing coaches in the right direction to ensure that they coach the game to be played in what we, the authors, feel is the right way!

It isn't a referee's manual, but it does offer opinions and thoughts on how they too can best enable the game.

It isn't an 'A to Z' guide to playing rugby union, but it is a blueprint as to how we can best play the game.

Neither is it a law book, but again it provides pointers to referees as to what and how to adjudicate. Last but not least, it is designed for spectators and parents to really enjoy this great game!

We, the authors, are two ex-rugby players who operated at decent levels of the game and who today, watch a lot of rugby that spans differing levels of performance, from Premiership and Internationals to amateur and school's rugby. During our preliminary writing discussions, a belief emerged between us that we were witnessing dangerous signs of terminal decline in the game of rugby union! That is a huge statement and one we felt required explanation and proposed remedies.

You will have noticed that we have entitled the book 'Lighting the Candle'. Originally lighting a candle was a long-held practice in many cultural, family and faith traditions. The practice is common across international borders and societies. The Chinese for example state that, 'it is better to light a candle than curse the darkness'. Lighting candles can bring serenity, focus and comfort to participants. It helps meditative thought when a person wishes to meditate on a thought or idea but lacks the ability to form the appropriate words to express themselves, lighting a candle is a traditional way to show the intensity of his or her thoughts and feelings. It is also described as an expression of support, where groups of people have taken up the practice of lighting candles to show support for many causes. The practice, when done by large numbers of people, helps build a sense of solidarity for the movement, as well as raise awareness regarding the cause. The practice began to mark a memory of a lost loved one and it is a centuries-old practice. The practice gives the candle lighter a specific time to reflect on the deceased, as well as to pray or meditate on their relationship with the loved one.

Obviously, the game is nowhere near as hopeless as that yet, but our concerns are real and considered. The book is a starting point for 'Expressing the need for solidarity behind invigorating and revising the great game of rugby union', in order to bring the game back to life. The book has been constructed to serve as a stimulant, a pointer and as a debating forum, providing an opportunity to take our views, consider them and thereafter debate them with our friends, family and colleagues.

If the majority of followers are happy with the game as it is played at present, then our concern is that we will see less youngsters being introduced to the game and the game itself being characterised by body armour, interminable time outs, thoughtless collisions, acres of space being wasted and individual skills rarely being evidenced.

It is also fair to say that another motivation for creating this book has been prompted by our experiences in the world of business. It has been written on the back of a number of business initiatives that have been successfully used in various consultancy assignments such as:

- Setting strategic focus;
- Creating relevant and deployable business plans; and
- Most of all, solving the eternal people puzzle. How do business leaders motivate, focus and deploy the human resources at their disposal?

All of these critical success topics have been included in carrying out various successful assignments that have been experienced, engaged in and deployed by SIMMERGY Ltd.

Organisations such as SIMMERGY Ltd. can give the required personnel the capabilities and, most importantly, the mentality and positive thinking to change the game for the better – to ensure that it moves onwards and upwards in a satisfactory and enjoyable format for all concerned.

Using SIMMERGY Ltd. as our commercial vehicle has provided a unique business perspective to peer into the game and its associated cast. It has enabled us to write this book about our rugby beliefs, including our keen desire to arrest any decline, real or imagined, through the identification and acknowledgment of the failings in today's game; and to provide insights and possible solutions on those things that can and need to be done, to rectify and deliver the game's values back to what they were always intended to be.

However, we are far from advocating a complete overhaul of the game. No that is decidedly not what is required! This is not forcing a draconian review on the game either, but we do believe that a few deft touches on the tiller by players, coaches and legislators will help the game develop for the benefit of all.

There are many messages to the game and some of them are key and more important than others! For example, 'less is more' is an important message; as is, 'don't over saturate the calendar' and 'don't make the game more or overly complicated' … keep it simple and competitive and a thrill to play in, referee and watch, – that's what we want and what this book was motivated by!

We believe that it is necessary to skim swiftly through the primary elements or essential foundation of the game, in order to provide positive suggestions as to how the game of rugby union can **improve**, for the greater fulfilment and for the enjoyment of everyone associated with it, as well as, hopefully, providing sufficient motivation to attract a new or wider audience into the game, primarily as spectators but also perhaps as players and officials? We also hope that it will provide some insight into the mind of the casually interested spectator, so as to develop his or her understanding to enable the gaining of a more rounded perspective from the spectacle.

This book is for those who care about the game; for those who desire to understand more about the game and for those who are ambitious to do more for the game. What we have tried to create in the following pages, are positive suggestions as to how the game of rugby can improve for the benefit of all associated with it. It is accepted that 'improve' is a relative term. In this context it is the medium through which all of us can experience increased fulfilment and enjoyment from the game.

Furthermore, it is to wrestle firmly with the issues of today, in order to secure the future of the game for our children, our children's children and beyond.

Throughout the book, the game of rugby union is described either as a whole or in its constituent parts. Included are creative ideas for developing, refreshing and improving coaching in order to make the game more exciting to play and to watch, as well as being safer for our children to play.

We critique the often, unnecessary, tinkering with the laws of the game aimed at making fundamental changes. This being especially relevant, as we believe that **what will genuinely result in change, is a mindset and attitude shift, to building rugby union into a game of skill and enterprise, not a game of attrition and collision.**

This latter statement is effectively the crux of our proposition. We witness World Rugby trying to bring about positive change, but their actions are muddled, they are often confusing and are often on collision course with the initiative released previously. A classic example of this is the reduction of the international calendar, closely followed by some three-year cycle of a Test Rugby competition.

Controversial issues are discussed, from the occasional lack of enforcement of the laws to illustrating the skills and the capabilities that are required to develop players, so that they can enjoy and deliver the fun that the game, has, should and can provide.

This book contains something for all manner of people; from experienced rugby aficionados to young people just starting to know the game; from the, often puzzled, spectator, who seeks to share in the ethos and camaraderie that the game gives in spades, right through to the experienced observer – both fervent and casual. It is for players and coaches at all levels; for parents and teachers; for the game's lawmakers and enforcers; for committee members and for sponsors and the media. Indeed, there is even something here for frazzled business managers, wondering how best to motivate and to challenge their people!

We have designed the book for either continuous reading from beginning to end, or, for selecting specific subjects, of particular interest to the reader, wherever they might be located in the book, to dwell on. The reader should be able to move in and out of the book at will and with ease. We also believe that we should explain things concisely and in such a way that it puts our thoughts and our ideals into the context of the game (plus the many "games within the game") that we hold dear for the future of rugby union.

Above all; it provides ample content to stimulate the necessary continuity of discourse among readers.

It is our ambition and our desire for all potential readers to be encouraged by our insistence upon:

- Positive thinking;
- Stimulating creativity in the utilisation of possession;
- Applying awareness to the use of width and space;
- Correlating techniques of offloading and the positioning of support players;
- Understanding the opportunities better that are associated with set piece possession;
- Introducing lateral thinking and peripheral vision as vital personal skills; and
- Developing the right attitude and approach to training, playing and watching.

As far as we are concerned, these are the key essential ingredients to great rugby, not just any old rugby, but great rugby.

We do address some of the more 'controversial' issues of the day – such as the much-discussed aspects of the set scrum, contact on receiving the high ball, the angle of a forward pass, and the involvement of the television match official (TMO). These aspects are all observed, analysed and solutions are proposed.

It is said by some that we live in an age of acceptable mediocrity, where an average performance is acclaimed to be of a higher standard than it actually is. Relating to rugby, this can be dangerous territory as we are perhaps comparing the game at different stages in its modern development over, say, the previous forty years.

There are too many variables applying to this debate (levels of fitness and finance are but two), but it is important that the general concept of standards as applied to, say, teaching, playing and spectating is scrutinised. So many areas within the game overlap one another when debating what the acceptable standards are that are applicable to the game being played at any given time.

Do we applaud that which is expected and give the players involved a false sense of achievement? Or do we remain mute and have the players long for some encouragement? We will discuss this.

Is this the age of 'collision' in rugby? Is 'Collision City' our citadel of satisfaction? Some love it, others hate it. Does it define a 'modernist' approach (along with 'acceptable mediocrity' and the law changes in the scrum)? For many good reasons it is essential that rugby's standards are raised. We only have to look at the number of parents who are worried about what's going to happen to their child in a collision to understand the need for clarification on this issue.

There is nothing wrong with seeking excellence – it is arguably the route towards at least acquiring acceptability. Parents of young players are looking for protection and a safe playing environment to be the hallmark of the game's standards. There is direct conflict between this and the type of game coached and played by the majority of its participants. This is discussed with reasoned argument.

Spectators, supporters and sponsors should be keen to be involved in the game's development and the lawmakers have a huge responsibility to all involved in the game to satisfy our appetite for greater enjoyment and fulfilment from the game we love.

CHAPTER ONE SUMMARY

The aim of this book is not to create discord,
but rather to promote positive thinking.

Will we succeed?

Well, we shall see, please read on ...!

SIMMERGY Ltd.

THE GAME'S FOUNDATION
POSITIONS AND POSITIONING

'Position yourself well enough and
circumstances will do the rest.'
(Mason Cooley)

The game of rugby has been renowned for its ability to accommodate all physical shapes and sizes, wide degrees of physicality and fleetness of foot or otherwise – up to recent times.

The coming of the professional game and arguably, the modern-day preconception of 'collision' as opposed to the general characteristics surrounding the game's definition as that of a 'contact' sport has required all players to be almost of optimum strength, to both give and take the hard knocks; now, apparently, the significant feature of today's game. This is, more often than not, displayed by the physical bulk of players – forwards and backs.

So, what has all this to do with players' positions and positioning in a rugby team?

Put simply, it means that players today at most levels are expected to multitask no matter their position – or, more to the point, their ability and their skill set (or their lack thereof!). They have to put in the hits and (with the protection padding aiding them) they have to take the hits, whatever their position. Yes, in times gone by, all players were required to tackle, but most players did it the way they were taught, around the legs, and usually a tackle was made by only one player – not two; one below the waist and another above.

So, physical strength per se is everything and certainly in the professional game much time has to be spent in the gym in preparation – usually on weights. It is our prognosis that perhaps 'gym work' has overtaken all other aspects of being ready, conditioned and prepared to play rugby. One hears, unfortunately, of teenage players suffering injury for various reasons as they overwork with weights and strengthening. Coaches and teachers need to take heed!

This backdrop of strength allows all fifteen players to be involved in the majority of actions within a game – we have props popping up outside the fly half to take a pass and they are expected to have the particular rugby sense to decide correctly what to do with the ball; and threequarters receiving the ball with little option (yet total expectation by support players) to drive into towering opponents and lay the ball back expertly.

The skill factor required in offloading and setting up a ruck or maul is essential, in order to retain possession. Hence, multitasking is no bad thing as long as it is not to the detriment of the standard of performance witnessed by the paying spectator. Alas, it often is! A prop in midfield, through no fault of his own, will not be able to maintain the speed of movement and, indeed the accuracy of passing, that is required to utilise space and width, as compared with a back – because, notwithstanding what has been said above, and with particular reference to ninety percent of players playing the game, they are not similar physical specimens and, more significantly, their mental attitude and aptitude are different – as we will now see when examining the respective positions in a rugby team.

This will be a brief overview to describe the foundational positions and to capture the imagination. It is far from exhaustive in detail, but it offers a general positional awareness. Just as in business, if the company decides to say, make an acquisition, the need has to be instigated by a business or by a market manager. Thereafter, differing financial perspectives need to be deployed from payback analysis to funding and transactional finance. Legal has a key role to play also as does human resources, including pensions and recruitment. This list can go on, the point being that many different roles make up a business team, just as in a team that plays the game. There are specialists and 'all-rounders' required, with everyone at least being familiar with and understanding the various activities taking place to ensure togetherness, unity and sympathy. This latter point is important as it's of no use for the backs to continually waste possession through kicking or, worse, dropping the ball if the forward pack are under pressure at scrum or line out or both. This commonality of purpose is what makes one team better than another whether it be rugby or business!

The following positional text is very much meant for the seasoned rugby person, but it is meant just as much for the concerned parent of a youngster new to the game.

To begin at the beginning, DIAGRAM 1 displays what the 'naked' pitch looks like when it is properly marked out.

DIAGRAM 1 – The Pitch

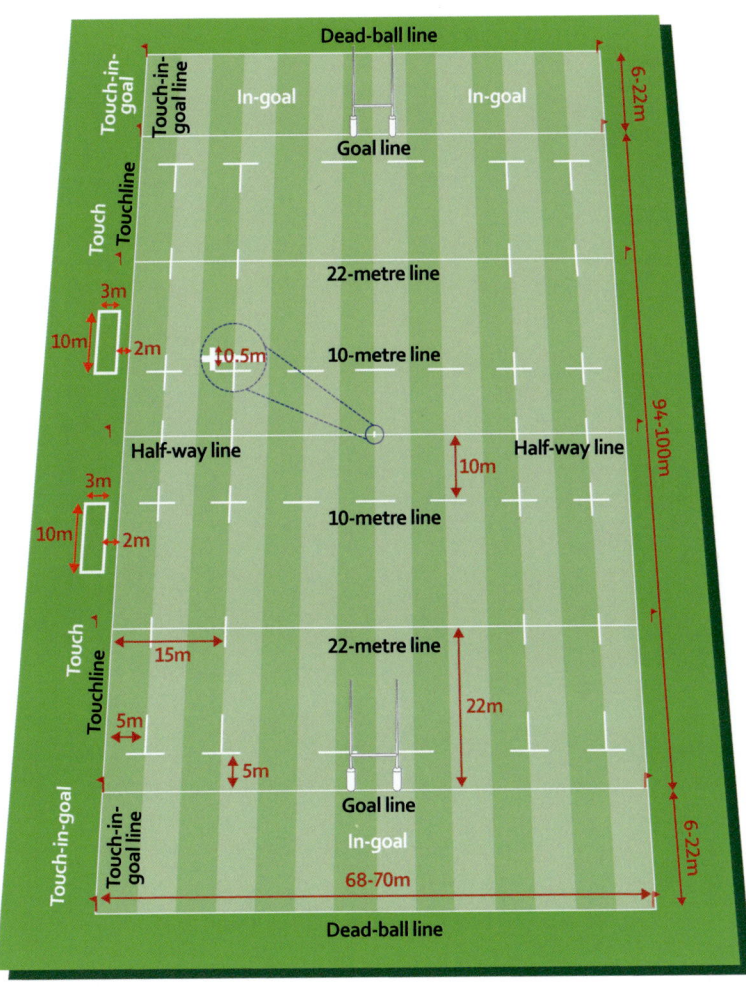

And DIAGRAM 2 illustrates the positions of the team on the field.

DIAGRAM 2 – Positions

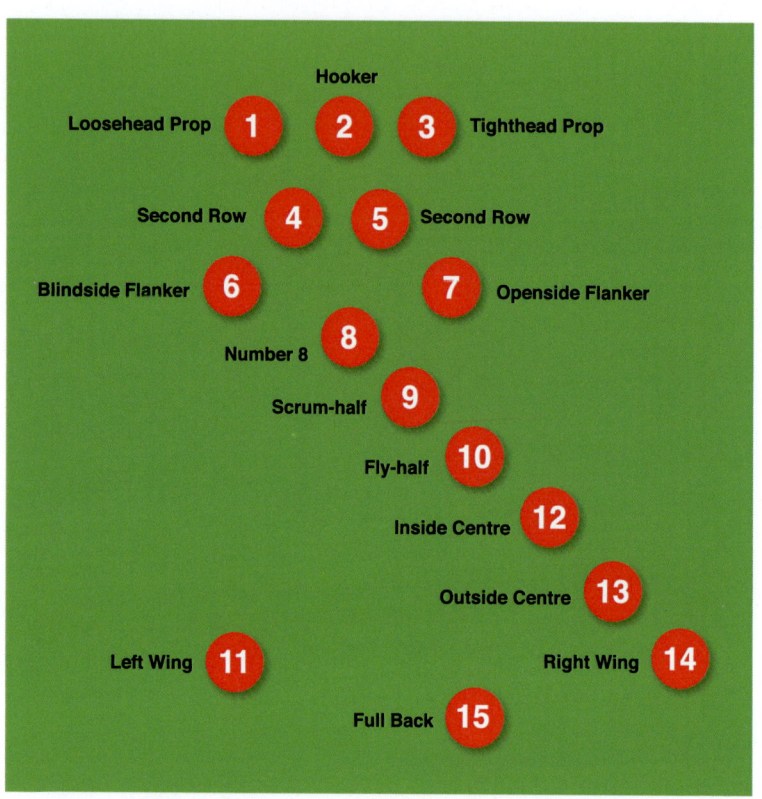

THE EXPLANATION OF DIAGRAM 2:

FORWARDS: 1, 2, 3 FRONT ROW; 4 and 5
SECOND ROW; 6, 7, 8
BACK ROW HALF BACKS: 9 and 10
BACKS: 11, 12, 13, 14, 15

This is the classic line up for the team, with numbers 1 to 8 forming the pack and the forwards; numbers 9 and 10 the half backs; and numbers 11 to 15 the backs, including the centres and the back three.

These positions, starting with the forwards, are described in detail below:

PROPS (LOOSE-HEAD – LEFT; TIGHT-HEAD – RIGHT) – NUMBERS 1 and 3

In the days when scrums were not such a shambles as they typically are now, the loose-head prop, on the left of the hooker, was blessed with sufficient strength to allow the hooker to see the scrum half put the ball into the tunnel for striking. It was all about technique, strength, co-ordination and timing – and more when considering the skill required from the other six forwards both in supporting their hooker and countering the tactics of the pack not putting the ball into the scrum. The props' body angles and sheer guts allowed the hooker to strike and the rest of the pack to correctly align themselves, depending on whether the strike was channel one, two or three – none of which are practised nowadays, with the game being the poorer for it, despite the opinions and advice of those who consider these tactics to infringe the bounds of the players' safety.

However, because of the scrum (even in its present confused state) and the line out (with the advent of lifting and ensuing driving mauls), props are required to be, arguably and all else being equal, the strongest members of the team, pound for pound. They can be on the move (along with the hookers, locks, flankers and number eights) for more minutes in the game than the backs, despite the interminable time spent discussing the pros and cons of scrummaging with the referee and taking time out for a chat before just about every line out.

Props really need to relish the 'one to one' contest of the scrums. Significant time must be spent in optimising strength and speed. They must work hard at the skills of offload and the techniques in dispossessing ball carrying opponents. They must be taught how best to support their team's possession from their peculiar starting point – being in front of the ball – at scrum and line out. They need to be thinking about what to look for in the opposition's defence of their side's movement of the ball – maybe they can see gaps laterally or in cover. Thus, based on what they see ahead of them, they can adopt correct running lines of support and their observation should encourage communication which will bring about appropriate collective judgement among the supporting players from the set pieces – in other words, they are beginning to play the game in front of them which puts massive pressure on the defence.

Alas, only about ten per cent of the aforementioned is witnessed among props at any level partly because they lack mobility, but mainly because they lack intuitive coaching.

However, while the days seem gone where a prop exercised a great deal of technique in the scrum, the advent of tighter defences (mainly because defence is arguably easier to coach than attack) has created many opportunities for the props (along with the hookers and the locks) to become integral parts of set pieces and counterattack. Whether they can add to their repertoire of side steps, change of pace and swerve for an outside break remains to be seen!

HOOKERS – NUMBER 2

Is this a misnomer?

The laws state that the scrum half should stand with his left shoulder in the middle of the tunnel and place the ball along the line of his front row. Then the hooker must hook the ball back. Some of the time they don't do this. In fact, typically the ball is fed in behind where their feet are placed! Arguably, hookers only have one specialist role, that of the line out throw in.

In a scrum, the hooker is today more like a prop and must therefore possess a prop's attributes. In a line out, it is natural for the hooker to throw in, given the other forwards' functions. However, bearing in mind the almost inevitable ruck or maul that follows a line out, the hooker is ideally placed to act as a blind side flanker, whether in attack or defence. It is the hooker who should be an expert at drawing and passing in the tight confines of the blind (narrow or short) side, where the use of width beckons, but which will only be successfully exploited by a straight running, skilled passer of the ball, possessing peripheral vision – all of which can only be achieved through simulating match conditions in training.

With regard to the throw in, there is no substitute for practise nor is there any excuse for the throw not reaching the jumper especially for those players who have hours to develop their game in the professional environment. The line out is one of the few areas in rugby where the side which restarts the game has a timing advantage over the opposition. Unfortunately, as lifting the jumper is permitted, it means that it is more obvious which jumper the ball is aimed for, but still the side throwing in does have the initiative if the thrower and the jumper (and the lifters) maximise their necessary skills – which takes a lot of time in the training paddock.

In describing the prop's position, we dwelt on the hooker, once upon a time, striking the scrum put in down one of three channels – between left lock and left flanker, between the two locks towards the number eight's feet, and between the right lock and the right flanker. This should still be worked on, provided that the set scrum can give sufficient support to the hooker as the ball is put into the scrum.

Scrum technique should be worked on to affect this added contribution that the hooker can make to the game.

SECOND ROW (LOCKS) – NUMBERS 4 and 5

Naturally, they have to be tall, as the line out has to be manned by no less than three potential jumpers who, although they will be lifted, must still be tall, as they must exploit height not significantly less than the opposition jumper, in order to maximise the advantage that the side throwing the ball into the line out has; This is a split-second initiative!

The front row players (the props and hookers) cannot be particularly tall, due to the scrum's formation and the flankers (and even the number eight) cannot have height as a prerequisite for selection, over other more necessary qualities.

The height and ballast offered by the locks at the set scrum is crucial to the mechanics of good scrummaging and their height and their strength should allow them to perform optimally at scrums without always relying on the number eight's drive from behind; due to this players sometimes have every reason to be binding loosely, pending movement from the scrum.

Because of the characteristics of the modern game in setting up broken play rucks and mauls, the locks' height and weight play an important part in producing quality offloads, taking more than one of the opposition out of the game when being tackled, thus sourcing an extra player in attack (albeit sadly underused nowadays), as well as taking and challenging restarts when the ball is in the air.

The locks need relative pace to optimise their contribution to breakdowns – pace to get there and pace for impact – hence speed just cannot be ignored in game preparation. This speed can allow the lock to play in the back row (blind side flanker or number eight).

Because of line out formation, there is very often a lock at the front of a line out who has not received the ball – presenting an opportunity to join the hooker in a sortie down the blind side, demonstrating qualities in straight running, delivering well timed passes and demonstrating an awareness of what is going on in close proximity to the play that is peripheral vision (PV), (PV is discussed in detail later in the book) and therefore enabling the player to respond accordingly

However, tall, heavy second rows can be so much more than big ball carriers ploughing up the middle of the field. The ball is so often in the air during a rugby match that it is ridiculous not to devise ways of utilising tall players more often. This is where the good coaches steal a yard. Restarts, the line out, high passes, failed kicks at goal and chasing high kicks ahead are all ways that the lock can be better utilised than at present; coaches, over to you …

NUMBER EIGHTS – NUMBER 8

At first glance there could be every good reason to assume that the number eight could be a third lock – except that in the scrum they are not bound in, unlike the locks, which allows them to be classified as loose forwards, along with the flankers (wing forwards).

In the line out on their own throw in, they sometimes move up and down the line, attempting to confuse the opposition. When it is the opposition's throw in, they tend to be positioned towards the end of the line, nearer the infield.

Because of their role in pulling the locks together at a scrum the number eight requires a great deal of upper body strength and being tall is an advantage in controlling the ball at the base of the scrum, utilising body length. In the line out, it is inevitably the number eight's height that gives a side the option of three jumpers.

The number eight's positioning in scrum and line out offers many opportunities to be a key player in attack and defence. A skilled operator will observe, judge, decide and communicate – all played out on the training ground – and will be involved in ball handling, especially from scrum possession and counter attack. Consequently, appropriate running lines in support are to be mastered, as are the many skills associated with handling.

The days of the number eight packing beside the flankers in a scrum – the flankers binding on the number eight, hence the three players being known as the back row – are few and far between. However, these three players form an integral hinge between backs and forwards, and the more often they play in the same team, the more likely it will be that they will get to know one another's pattern of play. This combination of thought and action is crucial in defence and attack and selectors and coaches will do well to work on the backrow as a unit.

Great number eights have the hands of a halfback, the strength of a second row, the fleetness of foot of a centre, sees all and communicates all, as the 'air traffic controller' of the game

FLANKERS (WING FORWARDS) – NUMBERS 6 and 7

There are two flankers within the back row (in conjunction with the number eight) and they operate off the respective open and blind (short) sides of a scrum and mainly from towards the back (and usually as the last man if it's the open side flanker) of a line out. This ensures that they tend to be the first forwards supporting backs in attack and defence. Hence speed is a prerequisite together with:

- *Intuition* – a combination of game awareness and acting upon reality will provide a sense as to what is about to, or can happen, within the next ten seconds.
- *Peripheral vision (PV),* which gives a sense of spatial awareness of what is happening and could happen (trouble or opportunity!) within seconds. *(PV is discussed in more detail in Chapters Four and Six).*

Flankers have the option of playing open and blind or left and right – defined by their positioning in a scrum. The faster of the two tends to play open in order to get to the opposition ball carrier (in defence) or a ball carrying teammate (in attack) as soon as possible. A great deal of pressure is placed on this player to make the most telling contact with the opponent (keep them on their feet or deck them), to perform the skills appropriate to the resultant breakdown (ruck or maul), or to be aware of how best to support (running lines and lateral or deep positioning) when in attack.

The blind side may tend to be not so fast (not slow!), may or may not be stronger (although it often is) – but must be the controller of this narrow side of the field from scrums and, along with the hooker, from line outs – not easy if the scrum's in the middle of the park! Thus, the ability to communicate with fellow players is imperative as are the skills of drawing, passing and exercising peripheral vision (PV) in relation to the opposition's drift defence. Peripheral vision (PV) is sadly lacking even in many professional players and we will discuss it later in the book.

The flankers must have a good general understanding of the game. They must possess a high standard of athleticism and they must demand for themselves total support of all of their teammates in return for the great advantage that they enjoy of virtual freedom of movement throughout the game.

It has been interesting to note the development of the flanker's role and the potential for this position to dominate great tracks of the game. The 'battle of the breakdown' as the new battle ground on the pitch has become defined. Therefore, speed to the breakdown (being first!) and strength to hold off the opposition has become critical. Investment in open side flankers today has often increased beyond the investment in tight head props and, indeed, standoffs.

So, that covers the forward pack, now for the halfbacks, the playmakers!

THE SCRUM HALF – NUMBER 9

It is difficult to identify any other player in a rugby team who repeats an undertaking more often, throughout the eighty minutes. The scrum half is expected to pass the ball from the base of a scrum most of the time the forwards win it. The same is expected from line out possession, as well as breakdown ball delivered from maul or ruck. In fact, nearly all possession secured ends up with the scrum half, who will most probably pass it to the first receiver. Is it because of all this bending that the scrum half tends to be the smallest player in the team?

A scrum half needs to:
- Be able to give and take passes, which may not always be accurate;
- Get the ball away very quickly;
- Be an accurate kicker;
- Be a good runner; and
- Be strong enough to compete with opposition flankers on occasion.

An eye for the break is crucial to create space and put pressure on the opposing back row.

It seems pointless discussing the scrum half's role at a scrum, other than to say that they are seemingly expected to flaunt the law 'requiring' that the ball be put into a scrum, as the law describes, at right angles to the touch line.

The scrum half is arguably the best passer of the ball in the team, given the requirements to do it so often and to get it in front of a colleague running onto it at pace (usually!). Foot positioning and the transfer of body weight is all important and it requires much practice.

However, it must not be forgotten that a scrum half with speed can cause problems for the opposition back row (open side flankers especially) and that a lateral breaking scrum half on a big open side from a set scrum having won their own put in can ask a lot of questions when angling in towards the opposition midfield backs.

Diagram 3 below, illustrates perfectly the important role of the scrum half in creating space and as a leader of the attack.

DIAGRAM 3

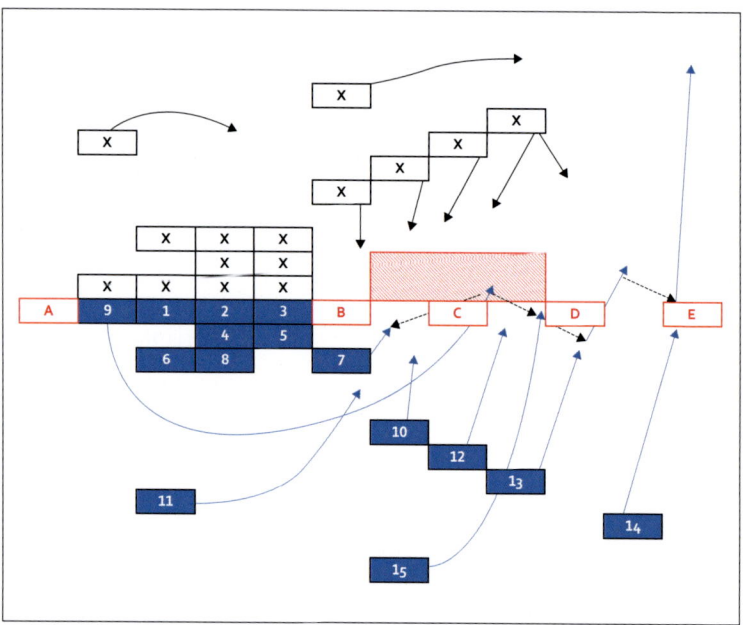

THE EXPLANATION *OF DIAGRAM 3:*

At Point **A** we see the scrum half (number 9) putting the ball into the scrum. As the ball is won and onto the number 8's feet, the attacking scrum subtly moves the scrummage to the left, Point **B**, thus nullifying the defending flanker. The scrum half runs towards and into the 'decision needed' space, as marked \\\\\\ Point **C**. It is here that the scrum half will cause the maximum confusion in the defenders' minds and also where the scrum half has the largest number of options of where to pass.

He can send the ball to his left to the fly half, number 10, or to number 7, or to the 'blind side' winger number 11 coming up on the inside; or to the centre number 12 going straight; or, as in this instance, to the full back number 15, who along with the outside centre number 13 at Point **D**, draws in the defending centres and winger, thus creating sufficient space for the attacking winger number 14 Point **E** to run on in space and score!

Another variant on this move is illustrated in Diagram 4 below.

DIAGRAM 4

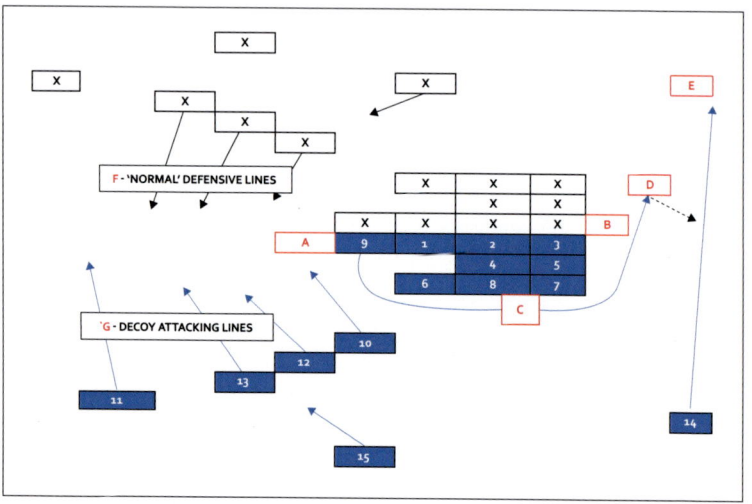

THE EXPLANATION *OF DIAGRAM 4:*

Using the same legend, here we see the scrum half (number 9) again putting the ball into a scrum at Point **A.** The scrum again takes a subtle lean to the left Point **B**, and the scrum half, at pace, picks up the ball from the number 8's feet, Point **C**, and runs straight towards the defending winger Point **D**, and releases a pass to his attacking winger in space to go on and score past Point **E**

This move is also helped by the distraction of all the other attacking three quarters lining up, as they are to receive the ball and at Point **G** cause confusion with "decoy attacking lines," which in turn, causes the defence at Point **F** to run the 'normal' defensive line! Fast paced scrum halves can make an attacking team very potent!

These diagrams demonstrate that the scrum half has a wonderful opportunity to create mayhem in the opposition's defensive plans. Quick thinking, pace and an eye for an opportunity are clearly differentiators of this pivotal position. However, it's not just passing and running that the scrumhalf needs to be highly proficient at. The higher the standard of play is, the more it seems to almost demand that scrum-half's kick into the box (usually taken by an opponent who counter attacks with relish having been literally 'given' the ball). Like the scrum half's passing, the box kick has to be accurate, and so requires much practice and also much discussion on training nights as to when and why it would be done in a game and, most importantly what the players around him are going to do; and who the kick chasers are?

FLY HALFS (AKA STAND OFF HALFS; OUTSIDE HALFS; FIRST FIVE EIGHTHS) – NUMBER 10

Teams are usually built around this position.
The stand-off is often known as the 'playmaker' or the 'quarter back' of the modern team; stand offs dictate the pace of the game, the team's movement around the pitch and they are especially, the key attack organiser.

Defence has to be done as well of course and so the stand-off must be able to lead the team's backline in defence and select the best defensive options.

However, great teams are led by great attacking stand offs and these players will lead the team around the pitch by instinct, intuition, sense and game awareness (hopefully, never by preconception!) and they will be able to make the choice as to how best to utilise their team's possession.

In certain circumstances, it can seem fairly obvious what has to be done with the ball. For example, probably a kick for touch (for safety) when in your own twenty-two metre area, but it is the surprise option that breaks defences down and the rest of the team needs to be on the same wavelength as the stand-off, who will often, as described, act on instinct and intuition rather than standard drilled-in plays.

There are always many options in all phases of play and the stand-off, as the team strategist, has the majority of the responsibility for making the right choices, and this decision-making capability is crucial and will determine the outcome of the individual 'play' and often the whole game's outcome.

The stand off's bias in playing comes from this instinct and previous nurturing, so it's important in selecting the player who will 'match' the style of play required, plus the other players around him. Teams with heavy solid forward packs are more likely to require many kicking options, so they need good fly half field kickers; whereas those teams wishing to play at pace in a wider more expansive style, require a fly half with impressive speed off the mark and great distribution skills for example.

Apart from this 'game reading' and game management capability the stand off's range of skills needs to be more complete than with any other position, with those of the full back running close. Passing, general handling, kicking, spatial awareness, game management, understanding of team members capability and insight into what the opposition are doing or trying to do, are all basic 'entry level' skills for the complete fly half.

That's the 'half backs' numbers 9 and 10. Now let us look at the three-quarter line and the 'back three'.

CENTRES – NUMBERS 12 and 13

After the forwards win the ball, they decide whether their team wins the game or not, whilst centres have the decision and the role to decide by how many!

This is the key determining role in any rugby team.

We will discuss the back three players in a moment, but these players, namely full backs and wingers, cannot 'win' consistently on their own without having good centres inside them. These positions need to have space and opportunity created by, primarily, the team's centres. This is the centres' key role; to create space for the teammates around them. They also need to run the defence, direct the attack and be central to moving the ball and the focus of attack.

There are many types of centres, not just inside and outside, there is the second playmaker type; the master of defence type, the crash ball straight up the middle type and the 'will-o'-the-wisp' type. All teams will have types resembling one of these four. What they all have to have in common is pace, excellent handling and distribution skills, plus the very real ability to seek out space for self and others.

So, centres are much more than 'outside flankers' – they need guile and skill to execute their attack and defensive duties, and they must be able to tackle well, to break tackles, to offload and routinely make the best of the space for the team, by not constricting it. So many centres close down space by running across the field. Centres have to run straight and make the pass or run decision right on the line, up close and personal to the opposition. It's pointless carrying out 'moves' fifteen yards away from the opposition, they need to be executed right 'in their faces'.

One word on space as far as the centre is concerned – it has been said that great centres on attack never, ever go outside the fifteen-yard line, because that's the winger's space. All the centre has to do is drag the defenders towards him, leaving the space clear on the outside.

THE BACK THREE – FULL BACK AND WING – NUMBERS 11 and 14 WINGERS AND 15 FULL BACK

These three positions are very closely linked, but it doesn't always mean that every winger can play full back, or any full back can play wing.

It is, though, correct to classify these three positions together because they are so reliant upon one another, both in defence and in attack. They are often the last line of defence as well as the first line of attack. Teams who enjoy the harmony, understanding and collaboration of the 'back three' will be successful teams and it is vital that they cover one another, that they support one another and that they consistently and constantly stay connected!

They also need similar skills.

Some fairly obvious ones are the ability to catch high balls under pressure, indeed, winning the aerial battle is a pre-requisite in today's game. They also need to be able to kick well and accurately. These kicks will vary from relieving kicks from deep to subtle little dinks and grubbers in attack. They need to be masters at exploiting space, both made for them by others and by making space themselves and for one another.

What is true is that opposition teams will soon work out where the weak link is and exploit it. If one of them is weak under the high ball (the Garryowen) then the ball will rain out of the sky for the whole game. If one of them is a poor tackler, that's where the attacks will be focused. And, of course, in defence, it is easier to defend an attack from the back three if there is a strong likelihood that one will not pass the ball! This makes the channel more easily defended.

They need to be able to:
- Link up together;
- Move the ball quickly from danger;
- Create try scoring opportunities; and
- Break through on rushing defences with power, with grace and with pace.

The back three have the role to re-start failing attacks, to attack from the deep and to go for the space with direct and oblique running lines that keep the defences guessing. Wide out linkman is a good description for each of the back three!

Perhaps most of all, they need genuine pace!

THE POSITIONING of PLAYERS' as the GAME DEVELOPS

The positioning of players' – both in attack and in defence at various restarts in the game should be reviewed regularly.

Here are two thought-provoking and stimulating, scenarios for coaches, teachers and players alike:

Halfway and twenty-two metre restarts
- Positive attitude – to secure possession;
- Necessary protection of potential receiver in defence;
- Necessary support of potential catcher in attack;
- Immediate awareness of pre-planned options of attacking side if catcher is successful; and
- Awareness of pre-planned options for counterattack if receiver is successful.

It is here that the contents of the following chapters play a critical part, namely –

- Use of space;
- Playing the game in front of you;
- Peripheral Vision (more than just visual awareness);
- Support (thoughtful, not thoughtless, and support needs to be physical not just mental, in the sense of merely thinking about it!); and
- Lateral thinking.

Back line formations
Why do backs mainly line up in a conventional formation? Much thought should be given to the positioning of numbers 10 to 15

- Lying very flat – or sometimes very deep;
- Options with the blind side winger and/or the full back positioned to run onto the ball from depth at pace or as decoy runners;
- Positioning the two wingers and the full back almost directly behind the fly half and two centres – for subtle playing off one another or as decoy runners – the potential variations are many and always certain to confuse defences

Here are some variations of backline formations for the coach's consideration in Diagram 5:

DIAGRAM 5

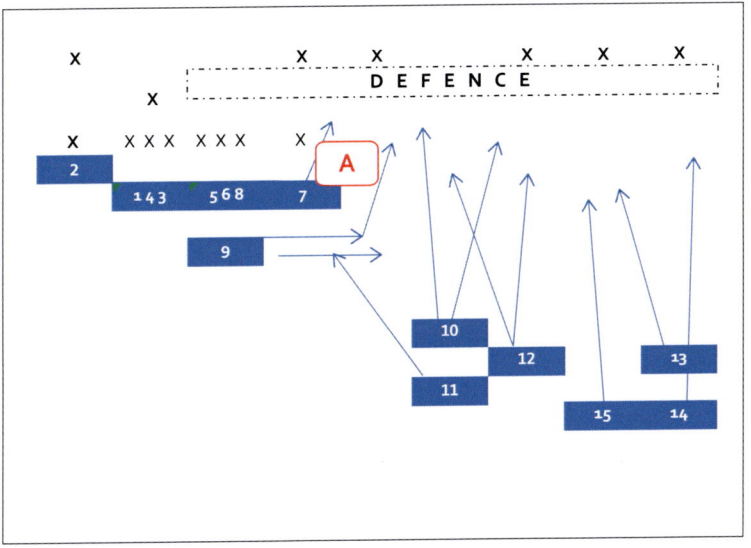

THE EXPLANANTION *OF DIAGRAM 5:*

In this instance following Line Out Point **A**, the blind side winger, full back and open side winger are all lined up directly behind the fly half and the two centres. On winning the line out ball, there are now many options or variations available, both predetermined and based upon the opposition's defending lines. This line up causes confusion in defences and provides much space from which to attack. In fact, alternative backline formations always cause confusion in defences!

In developing variations, the loose forwards or back row, numbers 6, 7 and 8 can also take up positions among the backs at any time during the game, where their presence can serve to create an extra player for potential overlap scores or where decoy running followed by vigorous support will create the overlap.

CHAPTER TWO SUMMARY

*... in which we have described what the pitch looks like and
how the players traditionally line up; what all the different positions
on the rugby field are; followed by describing the all-important
roles of these positions during the game ...*

The foundations are now laid!

CHAPTER THREE

ENFORCEMENT

*'It annoys me when people who don't know
what they're talking about, boo the referee.'*
(Jonah Lomu)

The laws of rugby are very clear.

Historically, they were well articulated and there is just sufficient room left for sympathetic interpretation, but little room for misunderstanding. Rugby union is a very technical game and thus the game has to be refereed with sympathy and understanding, otherwise it's just a mess of stoppages and infringement penalties and free kicks, most of which are not understood except by the most fervent of law technologists.

The referee is the sole judge of fact and of law during a match. This is the first tenet of rugby law and rightly so. This said, being the sole arbiter of fact and law is to allow officials to make mistakes, not to cover up errors. A concern is that popularity with players and coaches is intruding on the referee's only function, which is to referee!

In the world of business, managers often spout that what gets measured gets done. Regulation and control are important facets of business and simplistically this also applies to the game of rugby union. Let us just take a minute to consider these similarities; in business, the participants are constantly creating plans and strategies, and these are vital things to do. At SIMMERGY Ltd., we inform and teach our clients that strategy is not just about making a profit, it is more about beating the competition. Having a solid strategy provides the necessary framework to operate and to make informed choices. People in business must know clearly what they are definitely going to do, and also what they are definitely not doing. They also need to understand that there are often some things or areas that need to be worked out in respect of what 'box' they belong in.

It's exactly the same in preparing to play rugby: decide how we will beat the opposition, where their strengths and weaknesses are and how we will exploit the latter and avoid pitfalls regarding the former.

Players also need to have an appreciation of the laws of the game and be ready for a referee's interpretation of the laws and it is vital for the captain of the team to check this interpretation.

As stated, the referees' job and function is to control the game. It is decidedly not to coach, not to artificially let the game flow and absolutely not to be the player's best friend!

The great referees of our time are admired by players, coaches and spectators alike, and they are those who demonstrate this empathetic attitude towards the game and are always visible, but do not ever dominate it. They are keenly aware that they are not the spectacle on show, and neither are they the player's friend or best mate during the eighty minutes that they are on the pitch. They are the arbitrators of the laws and they are expected to enforce them without rancour or being pedantic or small minded. They are expected to govern well and to gain the respect of players, to ensure that the game is played in the 'right spirit' and that the 'governance propriety' of the referee is upheld and remains sacrosanct; always, always, always.

This aspect, along with the good natured 'banter' exchanges between rival supporters is, of course, what sets rugby union apart from all other team sports. It is a game with history and heritage, mostly connected with this, often indefinable 'spirit' are the law makers and legislators who fiddle with the laws at their peril.

In this age of professionalism and often intense media scrutiny, it has become important and necessary to introduce modern components into the game. This to benefit its greater athleticism, as well as any risks to welfare and fairness. Components such as the TMO (the third match official), citing officers, blood replacements and head injury assessments, are all important additions to the everyday game that enable the game to progress and to embrace the different times that we live in. However, there should never, ever be any sacrifice made to the fundamentals or base heritage of the game, or it will surely perish and die.

There is nothing more irritating to the paying public than the simple laws of rugby being ignored and/or messed with. Ignoring offences doesn't make them go away and sending every question or doubt to the TMO is not too great either. Adjudicating the game on the field of play are three pairs of eyes, the referee and two assistant referees, always within metres from the action. It is a fair presumption that for a lot of TMO referrals, one or more of the three officials can actually see better than the television camera, so they can police what's happening on the pitch themselves (for at least ninety-five percent of offences).

There are growing concerns that some of these fundamentals are being eroded on some altar of commercialism, and it has to stop, before the essence of the game is lost for future generations. Let us investigate and analyse some of the more immediate concerns ...

The Scrum

The scrum is the very heartland of the game. This is what primarily differentiates the game of rugby union from any of its close rivals. It needs to be competitive and aggressive and a real competition between the big, strong and hard men of the teams. The ball should be fed, by the scrum half standing square to the 'tunnel' into the scrum, straight down the line of the putting in front row and the ball has to be then 'hooked' by the hooker. Feeding, or putting the ball in crooked, with the aim to provide a further advantage to the side with the 'put in' is an offence, according to the laws of the game and should result in a 'free kick' to the opposition.

A clear and straightforward premise? You'd think, so wouldn't you? But go and watch any game tomorrow and see how this law is being ignored, at worst and corrupted at best. Most spectators hanker for a return to 'honest' put ins and referees who police this important law properly. World Rugby continues to make pronouncements on scrums and crooked put ins, but this is ignored consistently and deliberately by referees and players alike. The main issue is the 'scrum sequence' of 'crouch; bind, set' which is too often stretched out, takes too long and leaves front row forwards guessing at when the referee is going to invite them to engage. We view with horror what the declining rugby league scrum has become, and we fervently hope that the rugby union scrum will never come to that!

It is the scrummage in the game of rugby union which sets the game apart and is a unique feature. It should be a genuine physical and skill-based contest. It is significantly more than merely a re-start mechanism. Strikes 'against the head' are a rarity today and hookers are fast becoming third props, who throw in at the line out! There is ample sanction for repeated offences with 'yellow cards' being a sufficient penalty to stop the offences continuing.

As mentioned above, the other frustration of the scrum today is the 'crouch, bind, set' sequence which usually makes for reset after reset, and it is often a way of 'running the clock' down, thus being a form of cheating and short-changing the paying spectator. As soon as the opposing front rows engage, the ball should 'go in' (straight!) and then the clock should immediately be re-started and stopped again if it all collapses. The other 'game killer' for the spectator is the often arbitrary 'scrum penalty', being awarded for goodness knows what – half the time!

Is it too harsh to ask that opposing props who still wish to risk their necks and their shoulders by going to ground, that this is their issue? If props want to stay up and square, then they can! Front row forwards of the world should take this responsibility for the good of the game seriously. Wheeling, pulling or simply just not pushing straight, are easily spotted and should be penalised accordingly.

The Line Out

The introductions of new contemporary laws have cleared up the 'old mess' and have ensured that line outs are a much-improved element of the game today and with lifting permitted and throwing in codes prospering, there is real skill development in this area of the game. Long may this continue.

Where it is at risk is the allowing of 'not straights'. Throws down the centre line, no jumping across and no interference with the jumper in the air are vital elements to be refereed to keep this set piece honest.

However, if a 'not straight' throw is called and penalised, the game is then presented with the ludicrous situation of a scrummage being called where the ball is fed directly to the second row of the home scrum, thus rendering an equally serious offence to go ahead! This often occurs immediately after the 'not straight' line out has been penalised, as a solution to a crooked line out throw – ridiculous to any sane spectator!

The Tackle

When is a tackle a tackle? Interesting question and not always easy to answer:

If a player is tackled and goes to ground, they are not allowed to crawl on or merely get up without releasing the ball prior to continuing. The tacklers are often concerned about not releasing the player they have just tackled for fear of being penalised. If, however, they let go of the player, as instructed, he cannot be allowed to continue as described. There's a balance here and referees have to get this right, otherwise it makes for confused spectators.

It used to be that when you are off your feet then you are out of the game. Referee accordingly and don't allow players to 'dive' on top of other players on the ground, in the pretence of 'clearing out' a ruck. It ruins the game and it makes for a very unpleasant spectacle for the spectator and parents of younger players. After a tackle we arrive at the new battleground of rugby entitled the **breakdown**. This is where the ball is retained or lost with the other side's defensive alignment often scattered and confused. Therefore, ball won at the breakdown has become very precious. However, it has all the signs of becoming another mess, with players diving on the ground, over the players on the ground and making an unpleasant spectacle for parents and teachers watching. Gone are the days when the side going forward gets the put in and when you are off your feet you are out of the game. Enforcement please!

The Forward Pass

The most basic tenant of the game is that passes have to go backwards.
If a pass goes forward, then **IT IS A FORWARD PASS!** No amount of justification employing basic physics 101 outlining the case of two players running and a ball being exchanged or some gobbledygook about momentum or where the player's hands were pointing at the release of the ball in the act of passing … none of these 'amateur sleuthing' solutions, make the offending pass any less forward.

If the ball is caught in front of where the player released it, the pass is forward. Simple and obvious to all spectators. Stop trying to find some artificial analysis that can give a decision regarding the pass not being forward. This is not only irritating; it is plain wrong!

If a creature looks like a duck, quacks like a duck, has feathers, webbed feet and lives on the water, then, in all likelihood, it is a duck! Same as the **FORWARD PASS!**

There is on the field of play during any senior rugby match today, a referee, two assistant referees (who used to be called touch judges) and a TMO. There are also white lines and grass cut 'stripes' to aid the perspectives. It really isn't that difficult to spot ninety-five percent of forward passes.

Most spectators can spot them even if they are ignored a lot of the time. So, if the spectators can see a forward pass, why can't the assistant referee? Who, by the way, may just as well still be called touch judges, because currently their additional contribution is minimal!

Indeed, if the forward pass was refereed properly, the receiver would have to stay back and receive the ball, at pace, from depth. This, of course, has additional benefits, being, as it is, a vital rugby attribute and a cornerstone skill!

Offside

One of the most recent adaptations to the laws was to reinforce the position of the non-line-out players having to be back ten metres distance from the site of the line out. A similar situation was created for the scrum, stating that non-scrum involved players should be back five metres from the hindmost foot of the scrummage. In all other instances, players must be behind the hindmost foot of all ruck or maul situations. More than half a game can consist of attempting to utilise possession from breakdowns, rucks and mauls. The same applies for kick offs, no player can be in front of the kicker until the ball is actually kicked!

These offside laws were created to provide more space for the attacking players and if not enforced, perpetuators stifle the play and spoil the game for the spectators.

This is especially so with more than half a game consisting of attempts to utilise possession from breakdowns (the ruck or maul), this is where the laws need to be simple and easy to understand. It is with the ruck that the most confusion sets in. When is a ruck over? It used to be as soon as the half back had the ball in hand, thus allowing a constant re-positioning of the ball with the feet until it's just right to be picked up. At this point, the ball is usually kicked as it is now a terribly slow ball. The laws governing the end of the ruck have to be cleared up by the legislators urgently, because players and officials alike, are confused!

Teams today are highly intent upon closing down the attacking team as fast as possible. Plaudits are made to those teams who display and demonstrate their rapid line speed. This practice although exciting to watch when your team is doing it, does curtail space and therefore just has to be legitimate. How often do we see a defender reaching the receiver when the latter is only just receiving the ball from the scrum half? Basic arithmetic formulae confirms that the defender must have started from an offside position, as even Usain Bolt would have struggled to cover that much ground! The same goes for chasing kick-offs. These particular offside lines are clearly the domain of the assistant referee on the touchline, as they can see straight across the pitch along the imaginary offside lines, where the practice is easier to see – certainly most spectators can see when a player is offside in these circumstances.

Unfortunately, offside is often not refereed as tightly as it needs to be, and it is frustrating. It is vital that the implementation of the offside law by the referee and his two assistant referees is to benefit attacking, entertaining rugby. In many games, at present, the three officials are too often blind to defenders, either close to the ruck/maul or as far away as the outside centre, encroaching over the offside line – or, we may ask, do they see them and choose to ignore them and do nothing about it? By all means, allow defenders to defend on the edge, but when they cross the line they should and must be penalised. Once spotted, and penalised, we predict, for that game at least that creeping up early beyond the offside line will end and defences will be kept honest!

Later in the book, we offer ways and means for the attacking line to beat this close quarter defence, but it has to start with laws that are easily interpreted, together with switched on officials aware of their responsibilities to the paying spectators, the attack coaches and the future of the game.

A genuine plea from us, especially to the assistant referees – **Please, do your job!**

Yellow and Red Cards

These are adjudicating devices that many other team games admire and wish to use themselves.

However, let us remember that yellow cards were originally introduced to penalise and to stop consistent 'technical' offences, especially in the defending team's twenty-two or so called 'red zone'. Red Cards are there to penalise foul play.

Yellow cards are now issued for instances of foul play, primarily because the referee is intimidated or hasn't got the bottle to issue a red.

Yellow cards are there to clean the game up and to facilitate the referees enforcement of offences against the laws. No team wants one or two players in the 'sin bin' and coaches will soon stop selecting those players who transgress the most. Yellow cards are there to deter players from committing repeated technical offences that slow the game down and spoil it for the spectators. They are not there to be used indiscriminately or for the wrong purpose.

Red Cards should be like nuclear deterrents; because there is little doubt that the usual result of their deployment is a distortion of the game. They should be rarely used and only then for serious foul play; for the most callous or violent transgression of 'fair play'.

On both colour cards there is massive inconsistency by referees. Too often a red card is given for what can only be considered as a typical rugby collision; equally too often after a serious offence, merely a yellow card is given. These inconsistencies are not only irritating and controversial, but they do need to be rectified and eliminated as soon as possible!

General Comment

So as far as one can see, the enforcement of the laws of the game is sporadic and vague. Inconsistency is rampant and from World Rugby right down to the base-level amateur game fundamental laws need to be enforced, with sympathy and understanding, so as to engage with players and spectators to enable the full enjoyment of playing the game to be felt. But nevertheless, laws need to be enforced or outrage and cynicism will foster and eat away at our game.

In business too, there are 'laws' and whilst 'bending' and 'stretching' laws is often done, working in the world of business with an acceptable standard of ethics and staying within the boundaries of the law is important and necessary.

A final point for consideration; on the rugby pitch, is to ask – why can't the referee's communication system that he uses to talk to the assistant referees and the TMO, be extended to broadcasting their decisions, out loud, to the paying spectators in the stadium, a la American Football?

As a paying spectator, live at the grounds, you have no idea what the referee is looking at, what he has penalised or what his decision was based on. This is in contrast with the armchair viewer, who can hear and see exactly what the on-field referee is doing. Decisions are obviously also described by the commentator or 'pundit' as well, which may or may not be helpful!

The point being though, that as more and more games are televised, the spectators inside the stadium need to be looked after, at least as well as the television viewer; otherwise when games are televised, it will become better to stay at home thus reducing the atmosphere with the spectacle being 'live'!

Food for thought? No, this is urgent; so, get the broadcasts for the paying spectator made!

CHAPTER THREE SUMMARY

Chapter Three is where we looked at the need for enhanced
enforcement of the laws of rugby. They are 'laws'; not guidelines;
not please yourself directives; but laws.

Rugby union requires strict structure and strong positive
behaviour to prevent it becoming a mass brawl!

THE USE OF SPACE

'It's like everything in football – and in life.
You need to look, you need to think, you need to move,
you need to find space, you need to help others.
It's very simple in the end.'
(Johan Cruyff)

"Space, the final frontier ..."

Famous words that have an element of truth in the rugby context, because coaches do not spend enough time in getting their teams to think about how to create space.

You would think that in a field typically measuring a hundred and ten metres long by seventy metres wide that there would be loads of space for thirty players, wouldn't you? The base principles are that *defending* teams want to close down space as quickly as possible yet *attacking* sides (should) want to create and exploit space.

Therefore, the responsibility is with the attacking side to create the space and there is so much more to this than throwing out large mispasses which often cause as many problems as solutions. So very often, attacks are guilty of closing down space, because they don't spend sufficient energy, or time, in understanding what space is, how to create it and lastly, and most importantly, how to make the most of it.

There are those who believe that we don't need space in rugby. – that all we have to do is drive forward; make contact; pop up or ruck over; create another breakdown through collision with the opposition; and proceed up the field through security of possession and minimum movement of the ball. More often than not, however, this play does not progress up the field, but rather across the field, being fairly easy to defend and which is predictable and boring for the spectator.

The argument behind this line of attack is that sooner or later, the defenders will commit an offence and a penalty will be awarded or a gap will appear in the defence, allowing space to be utilised and, although far from certain, the attacking side will have extra players and due to an overlap magically occurring, will score. Sadly, even then, more often than not, this overlap is poorly exploited, such are the poor levels of skill sets evident among many of today's players.

Worse still, is the number of times the team in possession, with a large open side in the opposition twenty-two metre area, rely on continual attempts to drive the opposition back to their try line, only to be quickly decked and thrown back, time after time. There is little confidence in moving the ball wide; no understanding of how to straighten both the ball carrying and support running lines; and little ability to check drift defences (much less appreciate the gaps that such defensive alignment creates infield). The ball is moved wide only when the continual battering attrition has failed and even then, it is easily covered during most of its journey by the defence. Apart from delivering marginal success, this is so predictable and tiresome to watch.

On the training paddock, endless 'mini-games' of two against one, within a tightly confined grid, is where the essential skills are learnt. From 2 v 1, progression is to 3 v 2 and onwards to the full-blown game. Making space and neutralising defences are clearly what we have to develop in players here.

Here are some examples of how to and how **NOT** to, create and use space.

DIAGRAM 6

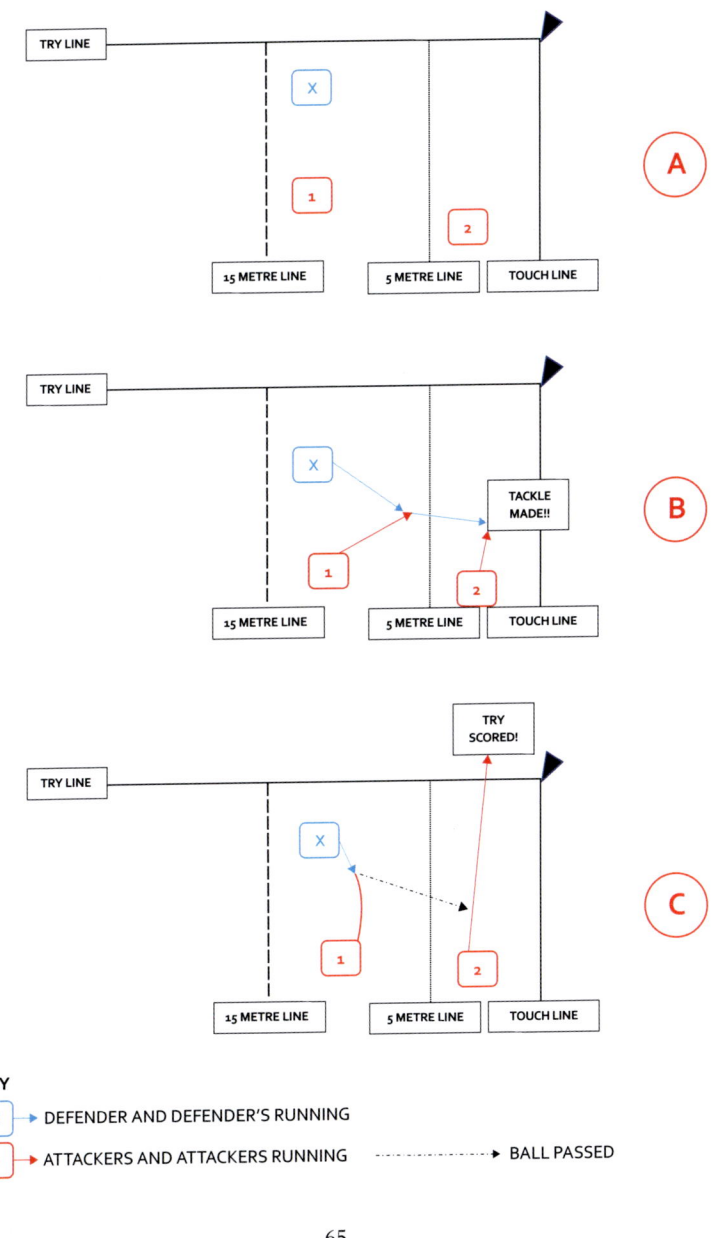

A

TRY LINE

X

1

2

15 METRE LINE   5 METRE LINE   TOUCH LINE

B

TRY LINE

X

1

TACKLE MADE!!

2

15 METRE LINE   5 METRE LINE   TOUCH LINE

C

TRY SCORED!

TRY LINE

X

1

2

15 METRE LINE   5 METRE LINE   TOUCH LINE

KEY

X → DEFENDER AND DEFENDER'S RUNNING

1 → ATTACKERS AND ATTACKERS RUNNING   · · · · · · · · · → BALL PASSED

THE EXPLANATION *OF DIAGRAM 6:*

Sketch **A** illustrates a typical 2 versus 1 scenario that happens all over the pitch. Players 1 and 2 are in possession and to score a try, they need to beat defender X.

In the instance illustrated in Sketch **B**, Player 1 runs across the pitch and uses up most of the space before off-loading the ball to Player 2. The defender X defends easily, and the try scoring opportunity is 'butchered' and fails.

Sketch **C** shows how it should be done! Player 1 straightens and 'draws' defender X, thus allowing a pass to be made to Player 2, who in open space and keeping depth, is far removed now from the defender and scores the try easily.

Sketch **C** essentially goes back to the basics of the game. The New Zealand All Blacks are the most successful of any teams when it comes to scoring directly from set pieces within the opposition's twenty-two metre area. This is what most of this book is about:

Possessing basic personal rugby skills, being as good in your position as you can be, understanding the significance of space and the actual mechanics of support. An ability to play the game in front of you with instinct and intuition to the fore and being driven by positive thinking.

If in doing the exercise shown in Sketch **C** above, note that it is a *'must score'* move and hard chastisement and extra practice should follow for those who do not score this way!

For those who appreciate quality, entertainment and added value, the utilisation of space at speed is arguably the greatest challenge in the game today (along with countering the demise of the scrum) and it also represents the greatest pleasure for the spectators and the players, who take pride in rugby being a game where skill and vision come way before collision and thoughtlessness.

It does not take a list of ground measurements to realise how much space is available to be utilised by the attacking side from a scrum or line out when two thirds of the players are occupying around twenty percent of the pitch. And even when play is moving forward from one breakdown to another, there is still about the same amount of space available, it's only that this space is continually changing and moving ...!

MACRO SPACE AND MICRO SPACE

At first glance, then, it can be seen that there is plenty of space available to be attacked or defended.

However, there are two kinds of space, namely 'macro space' and 'micro space'. The former is that which we have described above, and it is most obvious when set pieces are being set up. Unfortunately, this space tends to be filled too often by the boot of either the half back, or again, more often than not, this simply gives possession to the opposition, who can counterattack against dispirited, poor kick chasing defenders.

There is again, that commonality with the world of business. Any company worth its salt will research and work out where it is going to play; what size opportunity (market) there is, and whether there is room for a new business and its products, services and ideas. In business there is little point charging into a market that is already overcrowded, knowing that other competing players already have the business offering that you have, and they are already engaged and probably well-funded. They will take some shifting!

At SIMMERGY Ltd. we propose that when markets are perceived like this there is little point in trying to enter them; leave them alone and find more fruitful opportunities. This is really because apart from a long pounding battle, the primary entry tool in these circumstances is lowering prices, thus driving profitability from the market. Therefore it's not a good place to be and we strongly advise in these market situations, as we've stated, to leave it alone and find somewhere else 'to play'!

However, the business differentiator can, in these situations, be the exploitation of the 'micro space'! By adding something to the market such as the offering of other players who are unique and of value, a successful business can exploit this. A good example of this was the launch of the "Fever Tree" tonic mixers into what looked like an oversubscribed market dominated by Schweppes, but Fever Tree played the 'micro space' card of differentiated, premium and unique, which coincided with a veritable explosion in flavoured and botanical gins and thereafter, the whole market for 'mixers' grew.

The use of micro space and the challenge of the ball entering macro space in the hands of an attacking player are the real issues. Micro space is the gaps in defence when play is tight, either with a series of breakdowns or the backs trying to move the ball wide. Various contrived, pre-planned moves are attempted to create this space, but most of the time they fail because there is insufficient creativity or different 'plays' to confuse the opposition. Without this, the attack is easily subdued in micro space. This absence of new skills gives rise to the perception that it is easier to coach defence than attack.

However, remember that once the micro space is evident and once it is exploited, the attack is thereafter usually into the macro space which offers vast opportunities.

SKILL SETS

Basic skills, even at the premier end of the game, can be pretty dreadful.

There are players who simply cannot pass the ball accurately. So many passes go along the floor, over players heads or behind the player, stilting the fluidity of movement and attack. This is just one skill, albeit a critical one, in a game that is fundamentally about handling, but there are many other basic and personal skills required, not just to play, but also to utilise macro space. These necessary skills, listed below, can be assimilated and inculcated into all players:

- Slip or off load pass;
- Hand off;
- Sidestep;
- Swerve and a change of pace;
- Dummy and scissor pass;
- Draw and pass;
- Kicking;
- Create and Exploiting Space ...
... as well as sheer pace!

The application of these skills will of course vary depending on the degree of talent within the player ... some will always be better than others and some will have greater confidence to apply their skill set in pressure and in tight situations on the field. This is what sets the winners apart from the 'also rans'. The basic skill set that everyone just has to possess is the ability to pass well and an ability (and willingness) to tackle.

The effect of these skills being played out by the ball carrier can be the complete beating of an opponent, the half break which allows supporting players to take a short or slip pass (often termed an 'offload') and break a defence or commitment to the tackle by the defender, thus checking the defence and allowing attacking players to take subsequent advantage.

PERIPHERAL VISION (PV)

It is here that we introduce peripheral vision (PV) already first mentioned in Chapter Two, namely, the awareness of what is going on in close proximity to the play and therefore enabling the players to respond accordingly.

It is not easy for the ball carrier to know how the opposition is reacting to the attack, but the support players have ample opportunity to:
- view the defence alignment even at an advanced stage in continuous breakdowns;
- observe space among the defenders – observation;
- assess how best to exploit that space – judgement;
- communicate this to teammates – communication.

To get these to become the necessary, second nature skills, they should be practised at all training sessions. An attacking player's creative mind will beat a defender's reaction to the ball carrier.

No matter what efforts are put into building watertight defences, they will not stem the flow of intuition, creativity and high skill levels. Alas, it seems easier to coach defence than the utilisation of possession (attack).

Clubs and schools require their coaches and their teachers to be taught how to give players of all positions and ages (upwards of eleven years old) skill sets and peripheral vision.

Given this backdrop, players will be able to see gaps in defence, that would otherwise have gone unseen, and so micro space will be exploited, and the macro space, which is only a short distance ahead, can be penetrated, with a style of play which will give much self-satisfaction to the players, the coaches and the teachers and endless enjoyment to spectators and parents alike.

And, yes, there is of course still plenty of opportunity for collision. Rugby is, after all, a contact sport, but contact should mainly be made through the inevitability of the defender having to prevent the ball carrier moving forward and only occasionally when the ball carrier has no option but to make the hit.

Interestingly, peripheral vision is the hallmark of a good supporting player when a succession of breakdowns are occurring and a player at the top of their game in this capacity can spot the micro space created by the continuous, albeit varied types of, breakdowns.

DEFENDING SPACE

When we say that coaching defence is easier than coaching attack, this in no way implies that defence coaching is easy – especially organising the protection of the macro space.

This space can be very limited; for example, when the attacking side has a set piece put-in around the defending side's twenty-two. The defence coach must weigh up all the options open to the attacking side and he must be sufficiently respectful of their abilities to put into practice the aforementioned skills.

Initially, as in all aspects of defending set pieces, massive pressure should be applied to the attacking side's scrum and line out, as well as to the immediate movement that side will employ on getting possession. If the ball is subsequently moved wide, then defending players must move up ultra-quickly on the attacking side. The outside centre's positioning (as quickly over the gain line as possible) should be aiming to discourage the attack from moving the ball wide. Drift defence should be in operation, where the defender prevents the ball carrier from breaking inside while not committing to contact and thus forcing the ball carrier to pass to a colleague immediately outside, who will then become the defender's focus. This is worked very well by quality players, but it does tend to leave inevitable micro spaces infield which the attack should be able to exploit, if practising peripheral vision.

A problem area for the defence coach is when the attacking side is playing well and with growing confidence for whatever reason and the defending side is faced with, say, at least their own half to defend, with the game being played out around the attacking sides ten metre area.

Again, defenders need to be observing, assessing and communicating at the same time as trying to dispossess their opponents, or at least preventing them from moving forward. It is here when the defence wants to force the side in possession to kick downfield into the macro space (the defenders' half of the field). This kicking should be seen as the last resort, because kicking away possession is a problem as it takes so long to win it back again. Teams who are skilled at the 'kick chase' fare better in these situations than those who don't. In fact, a good kick chase can often turn a bad kick into a good one.

When the kick or box kick becomes unavoidable, it falls on the coaches to work hard on counterattack which, in a form of contradiction, is moving the play from macro space to micro space – not desirable. Consequently, a good coach will devise ways of sucking the opposition into this micro space for a short time, before setting out to utilise width from which macro space will be penetrated.

It is the same in business ... how do you keep competitors from intruding into your market 'space'? Some of the answers are to be found in exceptional customer service; differentiating constantly and above all, being an Innovator! Don't let someone else disrupt you and your business, get your disruption in first! Again, the similarities between business and the game are huge!

PLANNING - IN ORDER TO UTILISE SPACE

A growing number of coaches and teachers are using game videos in preparing for matches and practice sessions. It is here, if the operator is skilled and empathetic, that much positive work can be undertaken.

For the attack and the defence coaches to be made aware of what space is available at different phases in a game and to see how players in their respective positions react to attacking and defending these spaces, the video is an invaluable tool. It is a vehicle aiming to develop players optimally. It can be used, when viewed by players, to support these same players in their attempts to implement peripheral vision within the pressured conditions which they experience in game time.

Coaches and teachers must emphasise to players the availability and the potential of space; that any player can have this crucial ability to exploit space and that most of those players have to be on 'your' team to be successful.

This illustrates an important, core principle which is to never, ever or, hardly ever, take a pass standing still! Take the ball running straight, parallel to the touch lines, never 'across' the pitch, from depth and into or creating space ... in summary be creative, not predictable!

The skill of the 'off load', that is a pass given close up to the defender, with attacking players running straight into space is a very powerful 'play' in today's games and those excellent practitioners of this off-load pass, such as the All Black centre, Sonny Boy Williams, cause mayhem in defences and open them up for try scoring opportunities.

Of course, it should be remembered that attacking space is not just across the pitch, but it is also using depth, to come from nowhere and run unexpected 'lines'. It is also fair to point out that the best utilisers of space are accomplished in the basic skills of rugby, that is they can pass accurately and move at pace with ample support runners well attuned to what is happening there and then.

Planning can begin quite simply by the coach presenting a diagram to players of a set piece with a large amount of space into which his team can attack. Introduce it to the players and let them come up with ideas including how they think this space would be defended and therefore how best to counter that defence, that is applying concepts surrounding playing the game in front of you ...

CHAPTER FOUR SUMMARY

In Chapter Four, we have identified the seeking of space
as a core game requirement.

Without space there is no excitement or no showcasing of skills.

Creating and using space is the key skill in the game of rugby union!

PLAYING THE GAME IN FRONT OF YOU!

'The intuitive mind is a sacred gift and the rational mind is a faithful servant.
We have created a (game) that honours the servant and has forgotten the gift.'
(Albert Einstein)

Rugby as a game is an imprecise science ...

... it is fluid, alive and unpredictable. Often the best laid plans have to be torn up and replaced by a new set, there and then, while the game is going on. This ability to react and to change 'on the hoof' is the mark of the more successful team. This is what is meant by the phrase *playing the game in front of you!*

Whilst it may seem obvious that this is how the game is played, it is, regretfully, usually left to barbarian and festival type sides to play like this. Too often, tactics employed by coaches and players are too literally, 'play by numbers'; plays are set in stone, leaving no room for manoeuvring or adaptation and it usually end in tears with coaches trying to get a month's coaching instruction and changes completed in the half time fifteen minutes!

A vital aspect of the coach's job is to prepare their teams for all eventualities and to get the individual players prepared to adapt, to change and to go in a different direction.

People in business will easily recognise this aspect of their world. The business world is equally imprecise and 'things happen' that often cannot be anticipated or forecast, but nevertheless they have to be dealt with. When new managers are selected and trained, ready for the role of running the department, the team or indeed the whole company, they need to be well equipped to deal with imprecision as well as the more routine events. Regardless of what role the young manager is required to be trained in, training needs to include being prepared mentally and being clearly informed about what can be expected in the new role.

Secondly, what skills and capabilities are going to be required to make the role successful. In a new managerial role, the young manager suddenly finds that it is a lonely job. The American military training manual calls this the 'Loneliness of Command', and the more prepared the manager is for this, the better the situation is dealt with when it, inevitably occurs. It is very similar to the new player who is suddenly in space with the ball in hand the player has to know immediately what options there are, without too much 'thinking time'. This is only achieved through developing some kind of faithful intuition and instinct through rigorous training and thorough preparation.

A common habit in all teams is to decide to utilise possession determined by field location and type of possession (set piece or broken play) often known as 'pre planned moves' and inevitably communicated among players by codes.

There is plenty of good sense in this preplanning, but it is imperative that the way that the defence responds to the attack must be noted by the latter who has to show a positive response or, yet again, working hard at getting possession will be wasted.

This response to defence is what we mean by 'playing the game in front of you' and it requires a four-part sequential process, which we have named **OJAC** for short!

It comprises:
1. **O**bservation.
2. **J**udgement.
3. **A**ction required.
4. **C**ommunication.

It is important to emphasise that OJAC is more easily performed from set piece possession, as opposed to breakdown ball, as there is more reasonable space between the sides at set pieces.

However, get it implemented at scrum and line outs and coaches and players should be able to put their heads together to make it happen from rucks and mauls.

Easier said than done – yes! So, forget it – no!

Coaches set your standards high, apply the learning sets laid out in this book and to go that extra mile. After all, that is what you ask from your players, is it not?

When players supporting the ball carrier have completed this process then it is all about **LOP:**

1. **L**ines of support running.
2. **O**ffloading skills.
3. **P**eripheral vision (PV) – Spatial awareness.

Peripheral Vision or PV, as has been defined previously, as having the awareness of what is happening around you and responding accordingly. So, 'playing the game in front of you' is an ongoing process and a skill set in itself because it has to be undertaken when the playing environment is continually changing – executed in 'real time'!

Needless to say, many would strongly suggest that all this is unworkable, and they would argue that, even if they saw some reason in 'the game being played in front of you', it would take far too long to incorporate the practices required, in training sessions.

This is why it is required that it be introduced at opposite ends of the spectrum – at the professional level, where time is available (one assumes that most senior coaches are proficient time managers) and at children's levels, say, seven to seventeen, by club coaches and schoolteachers.

Coaches and players in the professional game may certainly argue that defences are so well organised nowadays that only preplanned attacks can beat them (usually conceived after hours of studying the videos of opponents' defences) – and, remember, it is easier to coach defence than attack.

However, attack coaches who can appreciate how defences react to utilisation of possession (videos again) can facilitate coaching 'playing the game in front of you' by employing the following methodology:

- Section off the field of play in a clear, concise diagram;
- Allocate potential sources of possession on the diagram;
- Make players aware of how best to position themselves in support;
- Make players aware of where defence positioning is likely to be;
- Identify any potential chink in defence at this stage;
- If identified, then decide how best to exploit it by using OJAC;
- If no chinks, then apply basic skill sets that can create space (*as described in Chapter Four – The Use of Space*);
- Get supporting players running off the ball to help confuse defence;
- Grid practice for players of all positions to apply the above;
- Simulate defensive patterns to create game situations for grid sessions; and
- All of this must be within staged development of game situations.

We also need to consider the art of counterattack, both in and outside the opponents' half. Diagrams 7a and 7b below start to describe this process:

DIAGRAM 7a

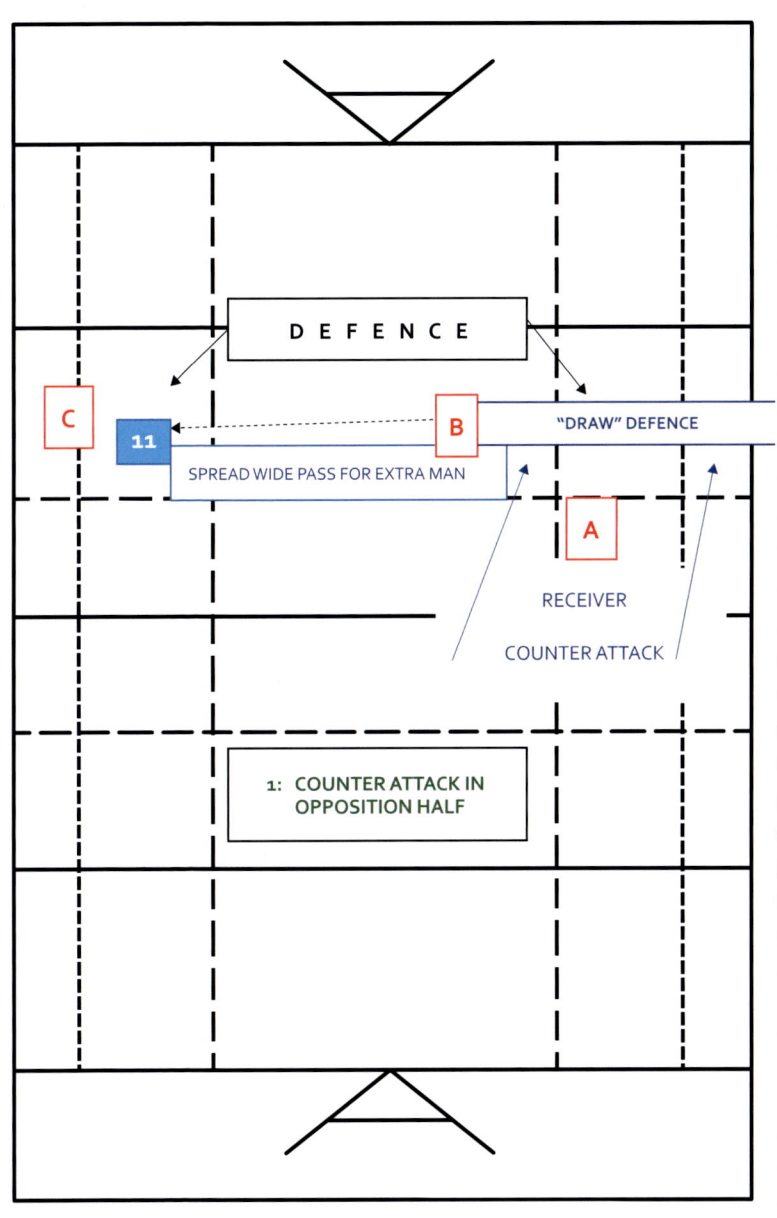

DEFENCE

C

11

B "DRAW" DEFENCE

SPREAD WIDE PASS FOR EXTRA MAN

A

RECEIVER

COUNTER ATTACK

1: COUNTER ATTACK IN OPPOSITION HALF

DIAGRAM 7b

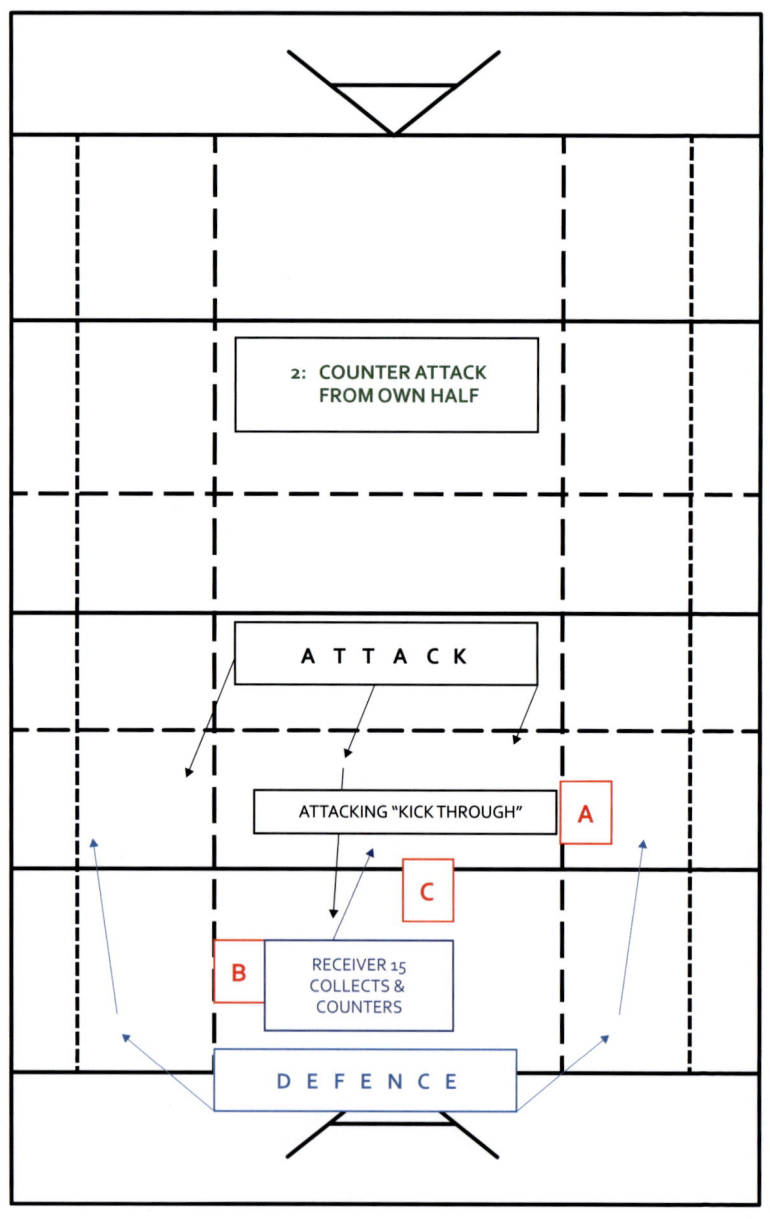

2: COUNTER ATTACK
FROM OWN HALF

A T T A C K

ATTACKING "KICK THROUGH" A

C

B RECEIVER 15
COLLECTS &
COUNTERS

D E F E N C E

THE EXPLANATION *OF DIAGRAMS* 7a and 7b

Illustrated above are two Diagrams **7a** and **7b** demonstrating the variations of the counterattack BUT with serious principles to be worked to.

In Diagram **7a** we see the counterattack within the opposition half. This is where players need to work at the ability to draw opposition into the counter attackers **A** strongly running parallel to the touch line and then once the defence is being 'drawn' at **B** and then send the ball out wide where there is space and where there is numerical player advantage **C.**

In Diagram **7b** we are now in our own half. The attacking team has kicked through at Point **A** and the defending teams full back 15 has gathered the ball at Point **B.** That Player now needs to get into midfield as fast as possible to Point **C,** as this will create two open side options to both left and right, with the opportunity to deploy OJAC to gain an overlap situation.

It should be noted that most counter attacks arise from the ball being kicked into an area quite near to the touch line.

It is usually at this point that the majority of thinking coaches may protest and say that they may well not have the time and/or the talent to put all this into practice. This is where we have to ensure that geographical locations throughout the country have sufficiently talented coaches who can coach coaches as well as, or instead of, players.

Respective rugby unions run courses for coaches and teachers to progress through stages of graded learning to enable them to coach the game proficiently at various levels from children to representative.

Set pieces, skill sets and secure defence are arguably, at least for those working with ages thirteen plus, the main elements of these courses that the aspirants experience. These are essential elements of tuition but tend to be rote based – and unavoidably so.

It is arguable however, that all things being reasonably equal in any game of rugby, half a team's performance will revolve around how well it recognises and positively responds to the way that their utilisation of possession is being defended against by the opposition. Therefore, it is vital that all courses for aspiring coaches and teachers include 'Playing the Game in Front of You'.

It may well be that it is difficult to integrate this into the courses' programmes and it is here that districts within countries would do well to appoint skilled personnel who can teach this specialist art – probably with the complimentary player assets of lateral thinking and peripheral vision, dedicating their efforts to coaches and teachers only.

CHAPTER FIVE SUMMARY

In Chapter Five we discussed the importance of intuition and instinct;
about playing the game as it ebbs, flows and evolves.
There are important rote calls necessary, but it is
more important to avoid trying to play like robots,
ignoring the realities occurring right in front of you!

CHAPTER SIX

PERIPHERAL VISION (PV) and SUPPORT

'Peripheral vision gave Wayne Gretzky his incredible on-ice awareness.
Peripheral vision helps race car drivers to know when to pour on the speed
and allows baseball players to tag a runner out as he slides into third.
Peripheral vision is important to your game too, no matter what sport you play.'
(Society of American Optometrists)

Having and using peripheral vision is a 'game changer'!

We have dwelt on this concept of the game previously, mainly in terms of players being aware of what is happening in their close proximity at any time in a game – this applies to whether the player is attacking or defending.

It is an essential component of defenders when the opposition has a formidable armoury when utilising possession. Also, it is critical to the ball carrying side when the defence is proving difficult to break down.

Peripheral vision is also known as visual or spatial awareness.

Googling 'peripheral vision' gives us, 'a part of vision that occurs only on the side gaze'. 'Vision' is defined as 'the ability to interpret the surrounding environment' and 'gaze' is 'the act of seeing' – all fairly straight forward!

The more PV a team attains the better it will perform. This is undoubtedly true as evidenced with the England world cup winners of 2003 and the Springbok winners four years later. The one thing that they had in common was that their backroom teams not only included a PV coach, but it was the same person, Dr Sherylle Calder

Many England internationals have commented very favourably on her contribution to their improved performances

The main benefit of possessing optimal PV is that it sharpens our observation, judgement and responses – remember OJAC? **O**bservation; **J**udgement; **A**ction required; and **C**ommunication.

Many will maintain that players either have it or they don't! This is very difficult for an average coach or teacher to impart PV to players. However, the same argument applies here as it does to the coaching of 'playing the game in front of you'. PV should be instilled into players from as early as possible and the 'seven to seventeen' corridor would be ideal. The time available to the professional coaches and players is sufficient for good planning to reap rewards regarding optimum PV understanding and implementation.

So, how do coaches at modest club level and teachers in schools go about PV development?

- They can obtain sports videos on peripheral vision. Whilst PV can relate to all sports, it may tend to be associated mainly with basketball, netball and tennis. However, it can also be adapted to the close quarter areas in cricket (batsman, wicket keeper, slip fielders area), soccer (quick interpassing on either approaching or within the penalty area) and, of course, rugby as previously illustrated.
- PV can be described as the player (usually the ball carrier, but not always) being aware (visual or spatial awareness) of surrounding activity, whilst looking pretty well straight ahead. So, create grid exercises where, for example, the player with the ball has the coach running alongside with a torch flashing on and off. This can be developed with the torch carrier running at various angles and with more players gradually added to the grid, by way of added distraction. Discussion among teachers and coaches, all of whom have a genuine belief that PV is good for the game, will stimulate the creation of a multitude of exercises.
- Advancement in improving what can be perceived by the ball carrier on either side will not happen overnight, but if this and similar exercises are practised and integrated into general game preparation, then the small group of players who have been blessed with peripheral vision at birth will be joined by thousands who will have acquired it through good rugby coaching.
- Coaches can develop activities for players to undertake at home, which will allow them to see more clearly (and subse-

quently correctly identify) objects that are moving quickly past them. The home computer can be put to good use for this.

- A major issue for the ball carrier can be assessing the distance between them and an opponent who is in their sight. The subsequent split-second decision will only be successful if the distance assessment was! Coaches and teachers should google 'Depth Perception' to get a good understanding of this, and to decide how best to devise coaching exercises to improve their players' spatial judgement.

The rugby union should be encouraged to seek out sports specific vision experts who are willing to invest some time in improving the physical vision of the rugby player and who can adapt knowledge and research to the game of rugby union. This group of crucial personnel – the coaches who coach coaches and the teachers to become better coaches and teachers throughout the country – will be empowered to instil, develop and optimise the personal skill that is peripheral vision.

SUPPORT

It may be assumed by many that the natural thing for a player to do in a game is to support – either the ball carrier or the defence of the ball carrier.

However, we know that the game is played very much around players' positions, which is a natural consequence of the laws of the game, so we must attempt to give players the ability to judge their positioning when in support, in order to maximise their contribution to the game and their subsequent satisfaction and fulfilment from the playing of it.

From an early age, players should be benefiting from their coaches devising simple games with manageable numbers of participants, in appropriately sized grid areas where space is on offer. Advice is communicated empathetically by the coach to the youngsters and there is an imbalance in the numbers between the two sides. That is, say, an extra one or two players in one of the sides so as to impart numeric advantage. The exploitation of this must become second nature to players from as early an age as possible. These types of sessions, with or without the imbalance, when devised by creatively minded teachers and coaches throughout junior rugby and continued into the senior game with the coaches exercising 'Observation, Judgement, Action and Communication', will instil in the players, no matter their ages, an understanding of where best to support (lines of support running), be it in attack or in defence. Then their positioning of the ball will be optimised for the benefit of their team and the game will be a better spectacle as a result – for the deserved benefit of the paying spectator. It should be emphasised that all teachers and coaches should either possess or be given the cerebral ability (would it be too offensive simply to define it as 'the wit') to create these sessions for the players to experience, no matter the age or the standard at which they are playing.

There is nothing quite so frustrating for the spectator as watching a game where players simply do not use the space to put their colleagues away, to score tries. How often we see overlaps ignored and opportunities going missing? These chances do not happen so often that players can afford to miss out on them when they do occur; and it's not just an unwillingness to draw defenders and pass into space for colleagues to run on to. More often, it's an incapability! Therefore, all clubs should have access to at least one coach who can impart the basic principles of peripheral vision and support – as soon as possible!

There are some key practices to train these skills and they are explained in DIAGRAM 8 below:

DIAGRAM 8

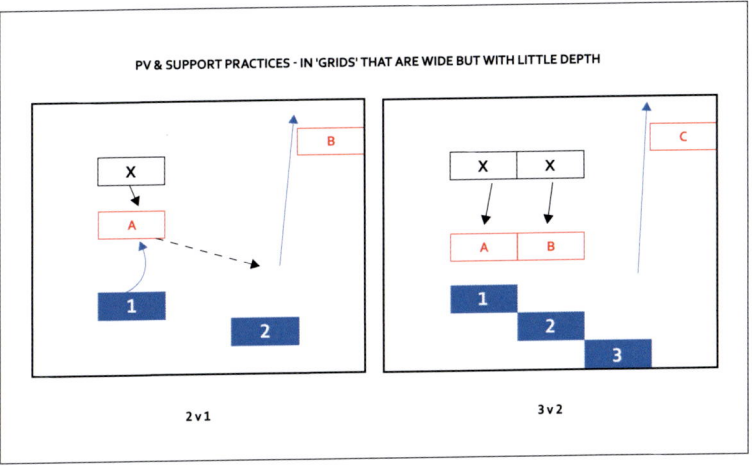

PV & SUPPORT PRACTICES - IN 'GRIDS' THAT ARE WIDE BUT WITH LITTLE DEPTH

2 v 1   3 v 2

THE EXPLANATION *OF DIAGRAM 8:*

The marked out 'grids' should start large and gradually reduce as players become more accomplished and confident. A useful size to begin with is ten metres by ten metres.

In order to preserve width and space, when it is at a premium, players are coached to run straight, or as we see in the first 2 versus 1 grid, at Point **A** at the opposing defenders 'inside shoulder', thus ensuring that the defender is committed to Player 1 who can then release the pass to Player 2 who is in space at Point **B**. Obviously, Player 1 can continue to attack if the defender isn't 'drawn into' Player 1.

In the second grid session, the players are increased to 3 versus 2, thus making the need for crisp and accurate passing higher. You can see at Point **A;** Player 1 is running at the defenders inside shoulder which is replicated by Player 2 at Point **B** dragging the two defenders into close proximity thus allowing the pass release to Player 3 at Point **C** into acres of space. Alternatives here to use are loops and misspasses as the players become more proficient.

Other key points to make is that the coach can control and dictate the defence in order for the attack players to implement 'OJAC' – **O**bservation; **J**udgement; **A**ction; and **C**ommunication. As players develop and also to simulate game situations, the players can be changed to have players of different skills, speed and physiques opposite one another.

In these training situations it is also good to set the players time targets in getting the ball to the outside 'free' man. This can also illustrate that while the misspass will get the ball there quickest; it will not draw in the defenders to allow the outside man to be free.

In short, the 'added value' to the player of peripheral vision is that it gives the player a choice – to make contact or not.

This kind of training provides the players with the **opportunity** to make decisions and it develops the **capability** to make the right decision.

CHAPTER SIX SUMMARY

In Chapter Six we discussed the critical nature of Peripheral Vision (PV)
and the crying need to support the ball carrier through the principles of OJAC;
plus, the need for teachers and coaches to be creative
in finding and creating space on the pitch!

CHAPTER SEVEN

THE HALF TIME REVIEW

'Don't give up at half time.
Concentrate on winning the second half.'
(Bear Bryant)

So, halfway through the book - half time!

We had set out to identify what we thought could be improved in rugby union so that all those associated with the game would get greater enjoyment from it. We emphasised that this should be based upon positive thinking in Chapter One.

Initially, we sought to highlight areas in the game which could be contentious, and which could lead to confusion (and, yes, boredom for many).

In Chapter Two we looked at the **Foundations** of the game which revolves around the players' positions and the subsequent physical and mental characteristics required from these players.

It is very important for teachers at schools and the coaches of young players in clubs (say, seven to seventeen) to thoughtfully move players to their appropriate positions, in order to match their talents and assets with the characteristics of the position. This will give them confidence and a greater understanding of their contribution within the game. Naturally, options should be kept open for re-positioning if appropriate. Parents should be informed of players' positions in a suitable communicative manner and also of what is expected of the player in both the set piece and in loose play, in relation to their positioning. This is not too hard to undertake, and it is sensible and responsible to keep a key person in the picture.

Enforcement in Chapter Three dealt with contention and confusion. They are not easy to resolve, but the scrum must be sorted out. It has made a mockery of the many values of rugby union which it, in itself, encapsulated, and has diminished the reputation of many referees, as spectators do not believe that the referees have sufficient knowledge of what is going on in the scrum so as to make correct decisions; and for three-point penalties to be awarded for relatively innocuous offences in scrums is quite ridiculous.

If the law is going to state that the ball can be put into the scrum approximately at the feet of the locks, then the whole technique of scrummaging together with its platform as a source of possession and attack has to be seriously reconsidered by coaches and teachers alike. This may offer massive opportunities for the game to be safer and more entertaining if the lawmakers and the enforcers get it right (so you have to make it easily understood please!). But is it against a fundamental characteristic of the game, namely, that the ball is put in straight, at right angles to the touchline?

In soccer, the ball is hardly ever out of play and consequently it is a game of speed and continual motion. In rugby union after much stopping and starting and restarts, there can be a further twenty percent of time added on for stoppages of one sort or another. Whilst the spectators enjoy being at a game, they are there, in the main, to see some action not to witness the preamble among officials and players. This lack of continuity should be a nightmare for coaches and players alike (or perhaps not!). It certainly adds to the boredom and the frustration among spectators.

In Chapter Four the areas of **Space** within which the game is played were then examined in relation to the utilisation of possession (and defence thereof), in terms of exploring, identifying and penetrating this space. Because of the relatively vast areas of space available in the field of play, as compared with that occupied by players, it was felt that it was crucial that we should introduce this subject early in the book.

Space is one of the most uttered words used by spectators, coaches and teachers – and more often than not with an expletive added! There is vast space at any time in a game of rugby union, begging to be exploited, explored and entered – it is by doing this that games should be won, but it can only happen by appropriate decision-making, the greatest virtue a team and its individual players can possess.

We expanded on this in Chapter Five and Chapter Six by introducing spatial awareness that is based on 'joined up' thinking.

It was natural at this stage that we illustrated in Chapter Five how best PV and support could be implemented in a game and we chose to encapsulate this within the strategy of 'Playing the Game in Front of You'.

It should be noted that the word 'strategy' is, in itself, up for question, as it could be argued that the side in possession is simply reacting to how the opposition defends or the way that the former is utilising its possession. This may well be a preconceived move that could be classified as strategy.

We strongly suggested in Chapter Six that **Peripheral Vision (PV) and Support** become essential elements of game preparation from an early age and that spectators and sponsors should encourage this, both for the added enjoyment of the paying spectator and for the increased return on investment of the sponsor. It is encouraging to see more national sides using PV personnel, along with a few senior clubs also. Let's hope that this creative strategy continues.

Let's return to the business definition of **'Strategy'**.
- Strategy is about making choices on where to play and how to win.
- It requires analysis on market, product, market trends, consequences and on competitor and customer behaviour. Coaches and leaders should be asking themselves: who are we playing, where, what are they good at and what weaknesses do they display?
- Then we need to consider what style of rugby we need to play and what skills and capabilities, indeed what players, do we need to play that way.

- How will the opposition react? Teams and individual players also need to be able to react to often unforeseen circumstances and events that can and do, occur, when least expected!
- In business, you really do have to 'play the game in front of you'; and the best managers who can succeed in this are often described as 'entrepreneurs', or 'visionaries' or 'creatives.' At SIMMERGY Ltd., we just prefer to call them 'well-prepared managers', who are holding all the skills required!

Not desperately far from the coach's job, is it?

However, let's not get too wound up with nuances! The attacking team is more entertaining, and it is utilising its available talent to much greater effect if it can read the opposition's defence and react accordingly.

So, being able to 'play the game in front of you' and total understanding of peripheral vision and support are essential parts of the first half of the book.

In rugby, as in business, it is important to be able to sit back and review progress objectively. At half time, it is important to recognise just what is possible in fifteen minutes. There is only sufficient time to make minor amendments to the tiller, to marginally 'reset', and concentrate on the current game's priorities. A coach cannot replace work that should have taken place on the training park in the precious fifteen minutes of half time. It's enough to highlight where the specific problems are but give the players no more than four points to focus upon. Clive Woodward, England's World Cup winning coach was the master at this, using his famous 'Flip Chart' in the half time changing room!

In business we call this adjusting 'on the hoof' and it is rarely successful for more than a short time. There will be time both in the boardroom or on the 'away day', as well as on the training ground, to fundamentally reshape the approach and develop the new circumstance requirements in skills, knowledge and capabilities.

Consequently, it is apt that the following two chapters on **Positivity** and **Lateral Thinking** are natural extensions to the first half of the book – demanding much thought-provoking discussion among everyone associated with the game, the outcomes of which would transform our game for the better, but which seem to be sadly missing at present.

Lastly, let's be clear … no trophy was ever won by merely leading at half time!

CHAPTER SEVEN SUMMARY

A good time to review and to reflect on what we've said thus far.
Well played (read) up to now!

So, take a breather, a half an orange perhaps and
then get straight on with the game (book)!

POSITIVITY and its IMPORTANCE!

'Your positive action combined
with positive thinking, ...
Results in success.'
(Shiv Khera)

Positivity is a rationale, created by an emotional state within an appropriate environment.

It is important to emphasise that the intention of the book has been to provide positive suggestions as to how the game of rugby union can improve for the benefit of all associated with it. In doing so, it has been difficult to avoid criticism and it must be emphasised that any critical views is based on objective appraisal of how we see the game played at present.

It is appropriate that, following on from the first half's topics from 'Foundations' through to 'Peripheral Vision and Support', we should build on that framework and now direct our attention to the power of positive thinking.

It was a privilege whilst compiling the book, to attend a talk given by the Australian rugby legend, Michael Lynagh. He showed a video of the last six minutes of the quarter final match in the 1991 Rugby World Cup between Ireland and Australia. Lansdowne Road erupted when Ireland took a three-point lead through a fine converted try by flanker Gordon Hamilton (interestingly comprising many of the skills we have already referred to in the book). Within minutes Australia had retaken the lead, Lynagh scoring another well worked try, to win the match; and they went on to win the World Cup. Interestingly, Lynagh is quoted as describing this try as 'the single best moment of my playing career'.

In his presentation, Lynagh, who had taken over the captaincy during the match from the injured Farr-Jones, explained how he had addressed his teammates while the Irish were taking their conversion. His mindset had encouraged him to dismiss all negativity. He refused to use the word 'don't' and instead used 'do'. He explained clearly what his team were going to do at the restart, where the ball was going, what he expected of the players by way of pressurising their opponents, and what they would do from whatever source of possession followed. Everything he had said was positive and it produced a positive outcome.

Keeping possession had been key as was moving the ball in plays that had been successful in previous matches. The players believed in their playmaker – this was imperative – and even when the Irish defended better than expected, the power of positivity that Lynagh had engendered in his players won the day. Of course, you need the resources to make it happen, but it has to be triggered by positive thinking. His on-field management of his players was creative and stimulating; his positivity being engineered through capability and reality.

But the talk that Lynagh delivered was to become even more poignant.

This same man, some twenty-one years later, found himself in a hospital bed in Brisbane having suffered a stroke. His initial feelings in hospital were encompassed by his thoughts articulated afterwards.

"I felt no self-pity, only exhaustion, and pain. At that moment, I was fully accepting that I was going to die in a hospital bed in Brisbane – no goodbyes, no hugs … I'd just be gone."

Fortunately, these emotions did not remain with him for long. The motivation of not wanting to continue feeling so ill drove him towards positive thoughts – towards recovering from the present and rebuilding a qualitative lifestyle.

His ultimate reaction to this unimaginable condition was not dissimilar to that when standing under the posts after the Irish try. Rather than dwell on what might be if he was not to recover, he began to plan his life where being positive would be the only route to any semblance of a fulfilled life.

REFLECTION

It is hoped that this book's content up to this point has been challenging, but also that it has encouraged readers to be positive in facing these challenges. Many of the issues which have been highlighted will find disagreement and others will be categorised as 'can't be done'. We believe that such negativity will ruin the game such is the strong argument that it is at present on a tipping point. Negativity and refusal to attempt to enhance the game for all concerned must be replaced by pragmatic positivity – for the ongoing healthy future of the game.

It is important to reflect on the various subjects within this book in relation to decision making on the field of play. They constitute joined up thinking. They might be new; they may seem unworkable; and they will probably not appeal to many. But if not energetically discussed among all rugby followers, then the game will be the poorer for it.

The business world embraces positivity more often than other factors. In the subtle arts of negotiation for example, managers are taught to 'Aim High' and 'Search for Variables', just as in rugby – believe that you can win and overcome the oppositions hurdles by maintaining a focus on probing for a weakness that can be exploited!

PLAYER MANAGEMENT and WELFARE

This short passage is aimed at the player's contribution to the essential skill of decision-making – a diminishing facet of the game; at many levels having been replaced by 'rote' (mechanical repetition).

We are not just referring to internationalists being given a sensible amount of game time throughout the season in order to avoid injury, staleness and lack of drive and motivation.

Serious consideration must be given to players coming off the bench in the second half – so called impact specialists – and the physical issues arising from their freshness, compared with opponents who have been under the cosh for at least half the game and usually more.

Coaches, teachers and parents must manage players of all levels and ages, in a way not dissimilar to that which gives any individual in society an acceptable work and life balance. There are many excellent rugby players who, notwithstanding their love of the game and time spent at it, find other aspects of life more (or just as) fulfilling and stimulating and who, indeed, benefit from having greater interests beyond the game – with this broader dimension adding value to their rugby prowess because they can bring this back to the game.

Good player management can underpin Sir Clive Woodward's TCUP concept. 'Thinking Clearly Under Pressure' revolves around decision-making, leadership and positivity.

Any player who can add value to their game brought from other interests and activities and lifestyles will be better prepared to contribute to this essential part of our game. Please note that players devoid of many or any other interests in life are still able to add decision-making to their skill set through good coaching and management.

Just as significant is the management and welfare of children playing the game.

The general levels of fitness amongst school-aged children has deteriorated over the past decade or so – this fact plays a signif-

icant part in the overall contact nature of the game, but also in the stamina levels of children, given the speed of the game now. Recent work by Bath University has developed a conditioning programme aimed at older children that also emphasises the importance of warm-up and getting bodies ready for rugby.
Being 'Rugby Ready' means that the risk of injury is reduced.

It is also worth noting that pupils at independent schools often play rugby at least two, three, four, five times a week, and with one or two fixtures a week, so they are 'battle hardened' or at least contact ready. Compare this to the state sector where sessions are run at lunchtimes or after school, once a week, meaning that club level is perhaps the only access a number of children get to experience 'contact' or full blown rugby and injury prevention.

A lot of current coaching practice now revolves around a game-based approach. It's very much pupil-driven, and the coach has become a facilitator rather than a dictatorial coach. The modern thinking is that pupils will perform better if they know 'why' they are doing things, rather than just regurgitating drills one after the other. Queues in drills are to be avoided and, given the diminishing attention spans of the current generation, action or activity is encouraged at all times.

It has been suggested that most skills, if not everything, can be taught through 'mini games' and, let us not forget, player enjoyment is very important to a lifelong love of the game.

In conclusion, as has previously been stated in the chapter, 'the power of positivity needs the resources to make it happen'.

This is summed up perfectly by the England attack coach, Scott Wisemantel:

"It is also about getting the basics right. Getting the basic skills perfect. The simple early catch. The ability to put the ball into space. The ability to run lines. Those things are important. That is what the All Blacks do well."

How right he is, and how similar to the contents of this book.

CHAPTER EIGHT SUMMARY

In Chapter Eight we have recognised that the power of positivity is the most powerful of emotions and facilitates the 'can-do' attitude required to win the game of life as well as the game of rugby.

The inner game is a critical game to win!

LATERAL THINKING

'Many highly intelligent people
are poor thinkers.
Many people of average intelligence
are skilled thinkers.

The power of the car is separate from the way
the car is driven.'
(Edward de Bono)

Lateral thinking or thinking outside the 'box' is a key element in the foundation for success in many competitive activities.

At SIMMERGY Ltd., we have derived a whole 'thinking' process because we realise that shouting "Think!" to anyone, whether they be colleagues, students, friends, family or rugby players, is simply just not enough.

You have to describe what they need to do to think and this is impossible! Thinking needs to be broken down into its constituent parts. It is a 'step by step' process that works back from the clear visualisation or verbalisation of what the end looks or feels like. From there, you can describe what capabilities were necessary to complete the actions taken. This, according to the research and consideration put in by SIMMERGY Ltd. is the only way to describe **Thinking!**

In business, it can create the unique selling point (USP), thus giving an organisation a competitive edge in its market. It's the added value that a social service has in supplying qualitative support to those in need. And it is the unique thought process applied by teachers and coaches to planning a game which gives that team the winning formulae.

One great certainty is that the so called 'intelligent' players, or ones who 'think' about what they are, or should be doing, will always outwit those with lesser intellectual horsepower.

Coaches, therefore, need to accept that intellectual or 'mental' training in a rugby context, is not only highly desirable, it is just as important as physical training. They are required to stimulate the intellectual muscles just as much as the vision, and skeletal muscles. This 'mental edge' development is to enable the players to work out what they are seeing and to ascertain the impact of what they are seeing, which is likely to have an impact on the game in the immediate coming seconds', or minutes' time.

To do this well, coaches need to describe the act of thinking in a more granular fashion. This is the real challenge! Thinking is a function conducted by humans every second of every day – but, as already stated, the nature of it is impossible to accurately describe or determine accurately.

Therefore, it is clearly not enough to bellow out "Think!" any more than it is to shout "pass, run, kick or tackle!"

There is a process for the rugby player to deploy; one that enables him to employ thinking as a competitive advantage. It is necessary to provide a structured approach to thinking that will enable each individual to consider those events that are either happening right now or are about to happen, right in front of the player.

This structured process begins by constructing in the mind, what the outcome of a particular play or game or move will be – what the end will look like? If we get this imagery fixed in the mind, it is easier to model and to create all the actions and the activities that will be required to take place to arrive at this outcome. Subsequently, to conduct those same actions and activities, some knowledge or a set of skills or capabilities will be required to execute the actions.

In summary, **THIS IS THINKING!**

These are those three critical steps:
- VISUALISE OR ARTICULATE THE 'END GAME' OR THE OUTCOME.
- DETERMINE THE ACTIONS OR THE ACTIVITIES THAT ARE OR WILL BE NECESSARY TO REACH THIS DESIRED OUTCOME.
- DEFINE THE SKILLS OR THE CAPABILITIES THAT ARE NECESSARY TO EXECUTE THESE DEFINED ACTIONS

Again, in a nutshell; define the outcome, acknowledge what actions were necessary to get there and what skills and capabilities were required to execute the action.

This is now the viable 'check list' for the coach that he can train them in until they are inculcated into the players DNA.

Many will maintain that players usually do not have the intellectual capacity to work like this. This is a complete fallacy! It is not, to coin a phrase, 'rocket science'! It can be 'trained in' but it requires planning and thought (a good coach's currency by the way) and although it may represent a very real challenge, it needs to be done!

Elements of this can easily be summarised or categorised as 'tactics' or 'game planning', but it is also the ability to equip players to think outside the 'box' as the game unfolds; as opposed to possessing blinkered vision and allowing routine to stifle creativity and instinct.

Let's look at some examples:
- Backs lining up in an unconventional alignment to receive the ball from a set piece or broken play. Very occasionally we see three of the backs standing directly behind a teammate which most certainly asks questions of the opposition's defence and very definitely offers a great opportunity for successfully playing the game in front of them. Obviously, this unconventional lateral thinking has to be backed up by personal skills and vision, all of which can be taught.
- Astute positioning of players who are attached to and adjacent to the breakdown, so that utilisation of micro space can be affected, stemming from the astute movement of the ball and subtly placed support players. This is already being demonstrated in the English Premiership.
- Create a team of players proficient at being able to run straight and draw and pass, thus utilising the many narrow side opportunities in a game and optimising the use of peripheral vision.

- Establish the ability within players to score when getting set piece possession within twenty metres of the touchline and thirty metres of the opposition try line, through well practised running lines, the demonstration of qualitative personal skills and the continual development of OJAC, in order to take advantage of the generous space and a defence very much on the back foot.

This should certainly be assumed to be well within the coach's standard game preparation script, but sadly, this is seldom evidenced, as players continue to run full tilt into opposition when the try line beckons, in an attempt to score tries through brute force.

There is a distinct inability among coaches and players to create the critical 'overlap' in attack and, at the same time, not being able to counter drift defence.

Hence, for the betterment of the game and certainly for the enjoyment of the paying spectators, we require coaches to apply lateral thinking to their game. It would seem nowadays that you have to think outside the 'box' to implement good rugby practice.

This most certainly seems to apply to the whole scenario surrounding set scrums.

We should all be making better use of players with assets that can rarely be countered, such as pace. How often do we note that it is these players who are, conversely, less mobile throughout a game than their teammates? More often than not we are referring to the 'back three'.

We have illustrated earlier in the book the options for the scrum half to break more often and test the opposition back row, rather than merely feeding the ball from the source of possession ninety percent of the time. They are not shutting down space by doing this but tying in the opposition flanker whilst being supported by their own number 7. The break can also be supplemented by the blind side winger, the number 8 and the full back, forming a further line of attack alongside the flyhalf and the two centres.

It may appear that the playing area will become congested that way, but it is not. In fact, it is being penetrated by creative, cerebral and pacey players outwitting a confused opposition and supported by teammates well-rehearsed in the OJAC disciplines, as previously described.

As much as anything, the competitive edge that a team has over its opponents is founded on the coach's awareness of the specific characteristics possessed by the individual members of the player pool – over and above their positional skill sets.

We have highlighted pace and positive thinking, but we can add values previously mentioned in the book, namely; those of peripheral vision (some players will naturally possess this more than others) and those with the ability to read the game played in front of them, employing observation, quick judgement and the ability to communicate the subsequent actions required to their team mates – all in the space of thirty seconds! Yes, even at a low level of the amateur game, there are some players who possess these abilities and who, therefore, can be counted on to lay the foundations for lateral thinking which will give their coach the winning edge.

So, please, coaches seek out the hidden skills, virtues and values that your players possess.

Diagram 9 below illustrates how astute lateral thinking can give a team an edge over its opponents.

DIAGRAM 9

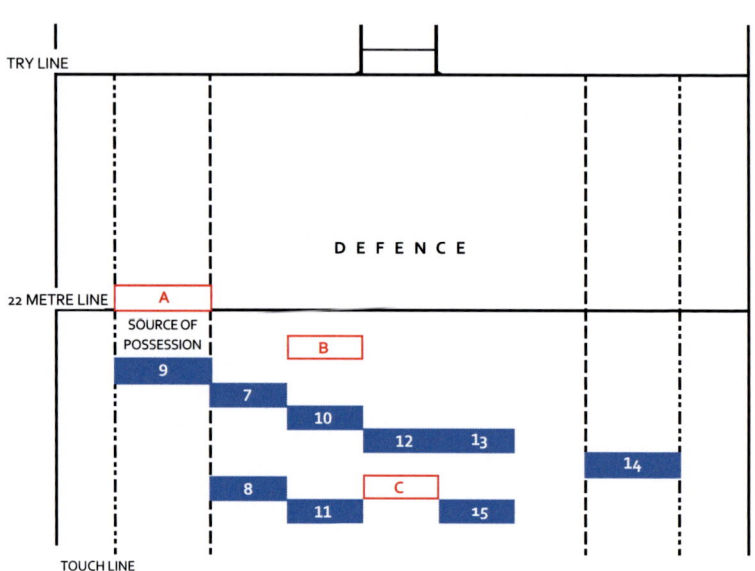

THE EXPLANATION *OF DIAGRAM 9:*

This 'multi option' or three-tiered attack illustrated shows that the ball is secured at Point **A** and distributed by the scrum half, number 9 at Point **B,** and then with a host of decoy and actual runners in midfield at Point **C**, disruption in the defence is assured.

This may seem ambitious or even unworkable, but is, in effect simply a combination of natural and purposeful support play, the utilisation of the players who have the most pace and the application of the principals of playing the game in front of you. It would be impractical if it were the framework for a predetermined move. It does require as many players as possible to apply positive thinking to the utilisation of possession.

Significantly for players, teachers and coaches alike, this three-tiered attack can be the basis for many other thought-provoking attack options where players can be better used, and so contribute more to the game.

And, last but not least, we would be **making optimum use of players with assets which can rarely be countered – Pace and Positive Thinking.**

CHAPTER NINE SUMMARY

All players have to learn to think!

*Thinking creatively – outside the 'box' – along with positivity and dynamism
is the most powerful sort of thinking that sets the 'greats' apart
from the 'average' and the 'good'.*

*Complex creativity executed well, will always beat mediocrity,
especially when mediocrity is executed in a half-hearted fashion.*

SIMMERGY Ltd.

THE FOUR Cs
CONTACT and COLLISION;
CHILDREN and CONFUSION

'Rugby is a wonderful show:
dance, opera and, suddenly,
the blood of a killing.'
(Richard Burton)

One of the primary characteristics of the game of rugby is contact – always has been and always will be.

Much has been written about contact and collision in the previous chapters.

Making rugby safer for those who play it now and will do so in the future, is a major priority for those who run the game.

Today, a growing number of spectators and parents of rugby playing children are complaining that there is too much contact. Medical staff are foreseeing the future of rugby becoming almost similar to that of American football where the amount of contact, having become tactical collision, would demand a significant amount of protection to be worn by the players, significant changes in the laws (being seen already in the scrum) and 'time out' periods, due to the interminable stoppages that are already pervading our game.

There was a time when contact was seen as a last resort – the only way to prevent a try being scored. Thus, contact was initiated mainly by the defending side. Now we have the ball carriers being encouraged to seek out an opponent and to make contact – hence we have 'collision'. It is not unfair to suggest that most of this collision is not entertaining – albeit there are always those spectators who go apoplectic at the hit! Perhaps this is a characteristic of the acceptable mediocrity that abounds in society.

It would be interesting to obtain the views of a representative audience (say, at an English Premiership or Pro 12 match – spectators, players, sponsors and coaches) regarding their opinions surrounding the way that the game is played today, including such features as:

- the stoppages for injuries caused by collision;
- the nature of these injuries;
- how the collision occurred; and
- stoppage for repetitive dialogue between referees and forwards before yet another set scrum is about to disintegrate.

What would the majority of those involved in the game today, say, when asked?

- Were you happy with the way it is played; are coaches and players getting satisfaction from it?
- Did you enjoy the spectacle enacted before you – spectators and sponsors? and,
- Are you worried or not for the youngsters coming through – teachers and parents?

If the majority of coaches, players, spectators and sponsors are happy with the game today then very little has to change (even they can't be happy with the scrum, can they!). So, the big question is – how do we bring more children into the game without their parents being understandably concerned about their wellbeing?

- Do we introduce contact and collision only at a predetermined, medically advised age?
- Do we advocate children wearing protective padding and headguards? and,
- Do we coach collision or contact on a gradual scale, starting with the basic tackle round the legs, head in the right place etc. and progress to seeking out an opponent and hitting them with the well-coached combination of venom and skilled ball distribution acquired during the teenage years?

However, if the majority want to see evidence over game time of personal skills, spatial awareness and optimum movement of ball and players, then is the foundation for this created by law changes, by sponsors' 'terms of agreement' or by ensuring that we have enough teachers and coaches possessing sufficient knowledge and persuasive powers?

The case for collision: Collision may ensure retention of possession, say, seventy percent of the time, but it does not ensure forward progress nor qualitative recycling of the ball. It slows the game down; it allows defenders to regroup and it requires little use of peripheral vision or lateral thinking – the very types of skills that gives a side competitive advantage when margins are tight (and gives spectators their monies' worth).

So, what are the main components of collision sufficient enough to avoid negative outcomes?
- Creating an extra player/overlap if more opposition in the resultant hit;
- Ability to offload (the skill provided) to the attacking side's advantage;
- Ability to protect the ball and avoid dispossession;
- Ability to make the hit at an angle to best minimise any disadvantage; and
- Awareness of whether to stay on one's feet or hit the deck if time permits.

It is here that we would do well to consider the game as played by children – and perhaps to be suitably encouraged!

One of the major issues in schools is that the current changes in the junior game, especially U9 to U14 age ranges, means that children's play does not mirror that of the adult game that youngsters see on television. Aspects such as uncontested scrums, no line outs, no conversions or kicks at goal may mean (in time) that it is hard for young players to have a rapport with the game. As such, this may in turn lead to player drop out, to pursue the many other options available to young people in this day and age.

The game of rugby is having to attract a new audience. In a world with so much going on, it has to, because there is a lot of competition for people's time! Thankfully, we are all much more savvy and up to speed with tactics, techniques, opinions and the joys of social media which means that good practice is easier to share amongst coaches/parents. As a result, any good coach will use these tools and their sessions will be better off for doing so.

Given the fact that the game has changed so much in recent years, the days of 'playing to win at all costs' has gone and schools that continue to adopt that approach are finding themselves very much in the minority. The days of 'smashing each other around' because that's how we used to do it, have also gone, with speed and handling or evasion proving to be more successful and more elegant methods. The adage of playing rugby 'like a man' and going through the pain barrier still lingers (especially when concussion is involved) but again, this is dying out, as coaches become more aware of concussion protocol and its damaging effects. Also, because parents become aware that not all their children will make the game as professionals, so enjoyment is more important. Skill and game awareness have to be seen as much more important than brawn.

It is current good practice for coaches to be silent and to use far more praise rather than chastising players at school or youth levels; focusing on what players do well instead. There is, of course, a balance for both, as by handing out too much praise, the levels of grit and the ability to take criticism drops in young players (possibly when the going gets tough?) but by maintaining a positive 'can do' environment in practice sessions may, in turn, lead to children being less afraid to make mistakes or to try new things. In short, coaches are trying to release the shackles and encourage creative freedom in a supportive environment, so that the young players can achieve and still enjoy the game.

However, there is no denying that some of today's parents are scared. The rise in statistics (and often not wholly accurate or applicable to all age ranges) means that there is a culture of fear around letting one's child start playing rugby. At a recent RFU conference, it was revealed that the levels of injury at prep school age in rugby are actually surprisingly low. The obvious downside is that some injuries being sustained in rugby can be very serious and affect vital parts of the body (head or neck for example) That said, by restricting all rugby under the age of thirteen, that means less playing numbers per teams, more time for the ball to be in play (by eliminating kicking, line outs and so on) means that the chance of a massive collision has been reduced, although, of course, any sport, exercise or activity carries a risk of injury.

Some media have not assisted parents who read reports by people employing scare tactics and they then want their children to stop playing rugby. In all honesty, give it five to ten years and many school administrators might see rugby only being played in clubs because of this!

Insurance premiums and compensation culture and staff being held accountable for injuries will perhaps only get worse. All schools of course have to comply with the RFU guidance (and in many cases the IAPS or similar) and this body is supportive, but there will come a time when headmasters might say, 'is rugby worth the risk?' Sad but true!

One issue at preparatory school level is the size difference that can be seen, especially at U12 and U13 age group levels. Take the example of a team who has the skills and the speed to play attractive, positive rugby. If they do not have the ability to compete at the breakdown and win the ball, then they may spend twenty-five minutes per half defending. So, size at this age level matters perhaps more than skill. That can't be right! But it appears to be very difficult to change, despite the fact that that is how it's done in New Zealand – there's a message here perhaps!

The RFU commissioned a survey only recently, to discover why young people play rugby and the overriding top answer was to play with their friends. Playing to win came out at number eight! Therefore, enjoyment is crucial and perhaps using a more sevens-based approach and having a less traditional fixture list using 'festivals' rather than the usual 'block' fixtures may make for more creativity and less injury. Those who wish to play more 'serious' rugby can then pursue this through the club system.

The balance for schools and the main aim of the RFU is to encourage 'lifelong participation' whatever the standard. Schools must ensure that the U8D team is as important as the First Fifteen, and this has started to filter down in schools over the past year or so, with more 'training matches' rather than 'competitive matches' being played – after all the children often aren't so concerned whether they have won or lost – the parents on the other hand … 'nuff said!'

As the children become older, things can become a little more serious. A good school will push their top players for excellence (and enjoyment) and encourage the weaker players to improve, have a go and just enjoy the great game of rugby!

Nevertheless, injuries (ligaments and concussion particularly) remains a great concern to everyone involved in the game. There are several advocates for changing things to reduce the incidence of injury and injury causation.

This, of course is creating an environment that necessitates the need to cope with confusion and disruption. In the business of rugby today, there is much talk about creating differentiated competitive advantage, and the people in business will search for new technologies and new ways of doing things. What often arises is the 'disrupter strategy', so called as the relative peace and calm of a market can be disrupted by agents who can't see any future promise or profits in maintaining the status quo. This therefore translates into rugby that says injuries and general unhappiness will continue to occur unless we all find a different way of doing things. It was of course, Albert Einstein who stated the oft used classic business stimulant to change; *"How can you expect different results if you keep doing the same things?"* ... a good point we think!

So, what do we need to change, to disrupt and to secure a better or at least an improved outlook on this repetitive injury problem?

Well, a good start would be to look at the sheer volume of matches being played at the professional level. This just has to be reduced, even accepting that no game equals no income. Professional players playing forty or more games a season are just asking for trouble on the long-term injury front; especially when the season goes on through summer tours and thus becomes a continuous, never ending season. Simply put, the game is placing intolerable strain on the bodies of those who play it, by asking them to play more and more.

The legislators are also having a go at reducing injuries through tinkering with the laws and, we suspect, making the game unbelievably difficult to referee. The best manifestation of this is the move to deciding that a high tackle is anything above the armpits instead of the shoulders. Apart from the near impossibility of refereeing this law, it will not reduce injuries. It may even make things worse!

There are moves to 'bring back the ruck' being led by such able journalists as Nick Cain. He discusses the old-fashioned proper ruck, not the static imposter littering the modern game! The neutering of the ruck could be described as the most damaging law decision ever taken. The key principle of the ruck was that the side going forward would win the scrum put in once the ruck had concluded. Therefore, all players were committed to win the contest for the ball. The aim was to stay on your feet, drive over and win the ball, resulting in a dynamic quick ball that opened up the game.

Removing this element resulted in large un-engaged forward behemoths standing in a flat-line rugby league style defence, ready to launch double tackles, whilst the ball holder is twisting and wriggling to get the ball back on the right side. With many matches today being played on artificial surfaces, where there is plenty of evidence welling up that these pitches are often the causes of ligament and tendon injuries, a double whammy effect on players' bodies is happening.

It is not difficult to work out or to contemplate for very long, why the incidence of concussion and ligament injuries have increased many times over is it?

As responsible citizens, we must not turn a blind eye to the recent well publicised issues surrounding dementia in sport.

Quite simply, as John Fairclough, the former Welsh RU surgeon says, 'the volume and nature of injuries need addressing.'

Sam Warburton's departure from the playing side of the game at a relatively young age is disappointing, this, together with Gareth Edwards wondering what the game will be like in five years, reflects the very issues that this book is addressing.

CHAPTER TEN SUMMARY

A chapter in which we accept that this great game of rugby union involves contact, but there are other ways to play and to win rather than bish, bash, bosh for eighty minutes!

And as the great Jean-Pierre Rives states ...

'The whole point of rugby is that it is, first and foremost, a state of mind, a spirit.'

SEEKING EXCELLENCE

'The will to win, the desire to succeed,
the urge to reach your full potential –
these are the keys that will unlock the door to
personal excellence.'
(Confucius)

The driving force in seeking excellence has to be the responsibility of the coach.

This is the first responsibility to the game, closely followed by broadening those responsibilities to the players and to the spectators.

In preparing to coach, ambitious coaches must avoid confusing their players and consequently, the spectators. That requires them to first and foremost get their thinking straight and clear.

We have tried throughout the book to promote and to motivate the thinking process that provides the right kind of outcome. It is exactly as described earlier in the book, that is:

- *When I'm finished with this team what will they look like; what does 'good' rugby look like, as defined by me, the coach?*
- *To achieve this outcome, what will I and the players have to do and accomplish?*
- *To complete this, what skills and capabilities will I and they need?*
- *This then, is precisely what I will learn, teach and coach! and*
- *I am now thinking!*

Coaches have to be clear about and to understand what they want the outcome of their work to be. Inevitably, this needs to be a granular detailed perspective, but the approach needs to begin with the big picture; for example, am I developing a kick and chase team; or a free-flowing handling team; or a defence orientated, 'score on the break' team or whatever the workable description needs to be?

Once this overall design decision is made, it will lead to decisions about what type of players are required and what skills and capabilities they need. Again, for example, there seems little point in selecting a 'running' fly half and then telling the player that his job is to kick all afternoon! This was the deep-rooted fault of the England rugby selectors in the seventies, who having done exactly that, then blamed the players for playing badly!

This very simplistically describes the cerebral work that is the coach's first activity ... Thinking! About what the aim is, in terms of playing style, the type of players required and the skills that they need to develop.

Basic skills on offer can often be pretty dreadful across the piece and the poor levels demonstrated by even senior and international teams are legendary. There are senior players, amongst backs, never mind the forwards, who simply cannot pass accurately. Too many passes go to the receiver player too fast or too hard, with little sympathy extended or not in front of the recipients, or worse, over and behind their heads!

The subsequent activities are therefore recommended in designing the coaching sessions. Clearly, there are some 'corporate' skills that every player needs to possess. These are the so-called basic skills required:

1. Catching and passing; under various circumstances. These circumstances vary from catching kick offs, catching line out throws, catching passes across the three-quarter line; catching cross kicks and so on. All catching relies on keeping eyes on the ball, preparing the hands and arms to receive the ball and getting the body position right.
2. Tackling from the front, side and back. Body and leg tackles, single and double tackles. Tackling big and small players at speed and slow movers.
3. Kicking: from free kicks to touch; spiral or end on end, high balls (up and under!) chips, grubbers; box, place, drop kicks for goal and out of the twenty-two. They all have their uses but they need practice in game situations.

All players need to have these basic skills, not all of them but the essentials for the position that they play in. A second row forward who cannot catch kick offs is of no use to the team, so this skill is an essential, and it is not just nice to have. The chart below illustrates these essential skills per position. Obviously, it is not designed to be overly prescriptive but, instead provides a basic framework of basic skills required to play in the designated position. It does provide an outline for the coach (and indeed, the player) to amend and to prioritise.

POSITION	ESSENTIAL SKILLS
Full Back and Wing	High ball catching Punting Front on and side tackling
Centre	Chip and grubber kick Parallel passing and catching Front on tackling
Stand Off	Kicking of all types Catching and passing Front on Tackling
Scrum half	Rapid pass and distribution from set pieces Box kicking
Prop	Passing and catching Smother tackling
Hooker	Ditto Prop plus throwing in to line out
Second Row/Lock	Ditto Prop plus line out catching Catching restart kick offs
Back Row	Ditto Prop and second row plus centre

We did neglect to put in verbs such as accurate, targeted, physical and so on, as the range of skills contained within each individual will vary, according to their basic talent, aptitude and attitude. The enlightened coach will understand the difference between average, good and great, just as much as poor and unacceptable. Clarity on what should be expected from each player and each position will 'raise the average' and improve the team continuously!

These make up the 'must do' elements of each position's base skill set and of course, their skill set can be added to as they develop and improve.

Clearly this base skill set should be viewed as an 'entry ticket' to the game, because without these skills the further key aspects of the game and how teams go about the business of winning, will never get done. It cannot be emphasised enough that working and polishing the basic skills of rugby, particularly with handling (catching and passing) under pressure, at speed, just cannot be practised enough. The so called 'added value' elements will never work regularly without excellent base skills. It is often stated that this is the reason that the New Zealand All Blacks have stayed at the top of the game for so long.

With these base skills at an optimum level, it then allows us to focus upon the added value skill sets of seeking out and using space; about looking for and executing the all-important 2 on 1's and 4 on 3's.

So, in preparing to coach the would-be successful coach needs to map out the style or the type of game chosen to play, select the team with the capabilities required to present and organise his coaching sessions around developing individual skills as described; incorporating them into unit and team skills and bringing them all into the collective whole.

The coach also needs to have the vital 'human qualities' to ensure success. These qualities are summarised as humility, enthusiasm, energy, great communication skills and being a disciplinarian, a networker and having the ability to extract the best from each individual team member.

A coach also needs to have considerable knowledge about the game. It can help if they have previously been a player, but not necessarily to have played at the highest level. This will help them construct their 'game plan' and avoid the usual pitfalls that we see from week to week. For example; field kicking without effective 'kick chasers' by more than one player is a recipe for disaster and causes more problems than territorial relief. A coach's advice should be to stringently avoid kicking the ball away, especially straight to the opposition in better situations!

In today's game, it takes so long to win the ball back from the opposition, why just merely kick it to them? Coaches should think very carefully about this and could, in fact, ban the entirely useless box kick for all but emergency exits from the red zone in your own twenty-two. Scrum halves are usually the worst culprits, messing about at the base of the ruck, wasting time and then kicking aimlessly.

As the late great coach, Carwyn James once said; **"kick to land not to hand!"**

The 'off the ball' running support is critical to maintain forward momentum. To do it well, consistently, the players need to be fit, agile and possess basic passing and catching skills. The rapid slip pass or 'off load' will penetrate opposition defences faster than anything else. This is a powerful playing proposition. Players who choose to walk and/or stand watching one of their own make a break, help no one and are useless in an attacking formation. It's not always the man supporting however, ball carriers who run across the field as opposed to directly forward cause supporting runners' nightmares!

In terms of going somewhere, say across the gain line, why do we see so many 'first receivers' receive the ball standing still? Why are they usually prop forwards? All they do is charge straight into the nearest contact over and over again! Stop doing this! The skill to be taught is to run straight, from depth and search for space or for a gap.

Be creative, not predictable

A coach is responsible for preparing the team, getting them ready to play. That they are confident, aware and physically motivated to play the game. So often the training sessions and pre-match warmups are dreadful. They are dry and boring and fulfil no useful purpose bar draining the players of energy and life. Make the sessions enjoyable, make them stimulating, and make them challenging. That will get the best from players and, most importantly, get them thinking! Indeed, why not use the ball, and develop the key ball skill of handling under pressure as part of their physical conditioning?

Whenever photographs or newsreels are shown of many international squads training, they tend to be doing something with weights or merely physical or gym training. When do they do skill work? Players need exercises that stimulate and foster the development of skills that are motivating and inspiring, please! … not more drudgery.

There are many debates circulating around the game in England about coaches and coaching. Not least of which is where is the next England coach coming from once Eddie Jones goes? There is an obsession with 'foreign' coaches being better equipped to deliver the kind of style and winning mentality that the home countries need.

In Scotland, the maverick, creative player Gregor Townsend, has developed into a practical and a very innovative coach of his countrymen. In England, we see the outstanding English coaches such as Brian Ashton (way before his time in thinking and style) Dean Richards and Rob Baxter. Wasn't Jack Rowell at Bath way superior to today's Todd Blackadder?

We also witness now that the savage experience of the 2012 World Cup didn't destroy Stuart Lancaster or Andy Farrell, it gave them hard experience to go with the coaching skills that made them better coaches – unfortunately only for Leinster and Ireland respectively, to benefit. Again, if we think back to 1999, wasn't Clive Woodward better for the losing experience in the quarter final to South Africa that year, thus setting him up for the glory of 2003? After 2019, Eddie will be gone and whither the coaching lessons for English rugby then?

Eddie Jones is building a reputation of injuring his best players due to over the top, intensive training routines, including wrestling. But isn't it a good thing that coaches possess an intense curiosity about ideas from other sports and apply these lessons to rugby? *Tactical Periodisation* is one such idea from the world of Spanish football (soccer) where four distinct 'game moments' – offensive organisation, transition from attack to defence, defensive organisation and, transition from defence to attack – are set up in sessions of training with systematic repetition of key theories that enable players to respond to pressure in the game easily and positively.

Dave Alred, who famously coached Jonny Wilkinson to kick better (mission accomplished we would say) was a coach who challenged conventional thinking. He was always seeking a better way of doing things across any number of sports. He has worked with Olympic athletes, Aussie Rules footy, the America's Cup team SoftBank and Johnny Sexton. He has also taken his unique approach into golf improving Luke Donald and Francesco Molinari's golf games, to name but two.

Even the best coaches, however, cannot do the job of the player, but he can entrust the on-field leadership to key lieutenants. It is necessary to build a players 'mental strength' as well as physical strength. A coach needs to see that readiness for the game with 'fight in their eyes' as the players leave the dressing room.

This mental strength is absolutely crucial. It enables teams to develop a 'we will not lose' mentality so as to always believe that they are better than the opposition so that the creeping inevitability that the other team will win, never ever, gets into the players' minds.

Again, this is an esoteric skill that people think you've either got or you haven't. This is also a fallacy and it is more than merely confidence. Confidence is a result of mental strength, not an ingredient of it!

By way of further explanation, there is positive and negative attitude and energy. Negativity is not a 'natural' function of the brain, it comes from bad experiences, then lingers and bumps-up into the positive or negative attitude an individual has. This can give birth to powerful currents of mental, and physical energy.

This chart below illustrates the point:

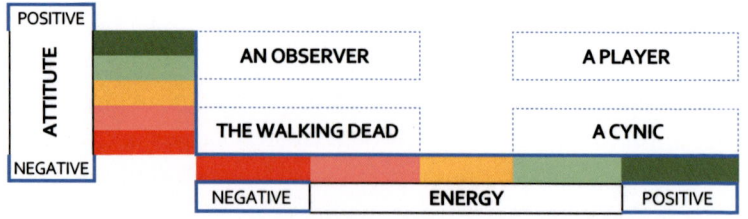

As you can see, any form of negativity, either attitude or energy, provides you with, at best, an **Observer** or a **Cynic** but more likely you'll turn into a member of the '**Walking Dead**'. We recognise them, in many walks of life, do you? More importantly perhaps, do they recognise themselves?

The coach's role therefore is to promote positivity at all times, because having a positive attitude coupled with positive energy equals **A PLAYER** – one that you can use, as described throughout this book.

Anything else will result in sub-par team performances. The 'rotten apple' story is indeed alive and well in most team activities from business to sport. These people are the type of player that any team, at any level, just does not need!

Suffice it to say therefore, whether dealing with a skilled rugby player, psychologist, friend, therapist, doctor or strategist, a rugby coach's job is multi-layered and complex. Just like a field commander on the battlefield, the successful coach will always make sense out of the noise and chaos generated by a team of rugby players!

For example …

HOW MANY WAYS CAN A COACH SAY "GET THE BALL & SCORE SOME POINTS!"

CHAPTER ELEVEN SUMMARY

Chapter Eleven is where we have learnt that
the search for excellence never ends.

Coaches need to visualise what excellence looks like and to work things out in
terms of what actions, skills and practices that we need to promote to get to
what we term today as excellent.

Then we need to re-set the dial, seek out and go on to the next level.

Continuous improvement is the vital 'call to arms' for all players!

CHAPTER TWELVE

THE FUTURE

'Good, better, best. Never let it rest.
'Til your good is better and your better is best.'
(St. Jerome)

'Dear Past, thank you for all the lessons.
Dear Future, I am ready!'
(Anonymous)

So, what does this all mean?

We've discussed many things and we have aligned the thinking of the rugby union with the world of business.

We should appreciate the many demands on all of us connected with the game. All experienced military commanders inform us that the great leaders on the battlefields are those who can make sense out of the noise and the chaos surrounding them.

In this book, we have transferred the SIMMERGY Ltd. process that enables people to think more clearly and to think smarter, so as to get to the heart of the matter. One thing, as sure as eggs, is that we mustn't ever forget that it is people who get things done, so everyone concerned with rugby, as in business, should support and enable the people whether they be players, referees, legislators or spectators.

Throughout this book, we have aimed for a switch in philosophy within the game, spearheaded by coaches and embraced by players and legislators and subsequently enjoyed by spectators. In Chapter Ten we discussed the issue around bringing children through the age groups into a lifetime of participation in the game. We talked about selecting teams by size and weight, rather than by age, to enable the development of positivity and skill; even perhaps utilising the culture of the sevens to help this.

Ben Ryan the leading sevens coach who took Fiji to Olympic Gold in the sevens in 2016, says:

"In the southern hemisphere it is easier to flip from XV's to 7's as it is more of an athletic, open game. Whereas the English premiership at the moment with less skills and more power, is more attritional, it is about keeping the ball over multi phases.

If we envisage how the XV's game will go in the next few years it is going to go one of two ways. If we don't get a grip on the laws around breakdowns, we are going to have even bigger players, more collisions and more injuries. But, if we put more of a slant onto skills, then we will see a more athletic game that 7's is closer to."

This, of course, reinforces a central message of this book ... let's get skilful and creative, not be builders of mass and cudgels. This is better for spectators, better for players, especially those starting off in the game at nine, ten and eleven years of age, there will be less injuries and an overall improvement in enjoyment for all!

Essentially, we think that rugby union is the king of all team games. It builds camaraderie and friendships that remain in place for years, often for ever. The banter and the anecdotes become legends. This all applies whatever level you have played at, from representing your school U13's as a reserve winger to gracing the turf in an international stadium, as a full-blown International player. The game fosters loyalty, discipline and appreciation that diversity is good. We, the authors of this narrative, can easily point to lasting friendships across this great divide; to funny and arresting stories of fortitude and desperation that have affected us and the people who we know.

Every year the game gets stronger and, with that evolution, often the frustrations and the irritations with the law makers, the law enforcers, the influence of 'soccer' grows too. We all have a responsibility to those who went before, to maintain the almost indefinable spirit of the game and to keep all things that are meaningful and precious to the heritage and the legacy of the game. Of course, we cannot live in the dark ages; the game must become contemporary and attractive for forthcoming generations. We firmly believe that it can do that without losing the essence and the spirit of the game. Without this, it will merely descend into a wrestling match with a ball!

So, where do we go next? What is the future for this game of ours?

With professionalism growing, funding remaining tight, the growth of the world game as illustrated by the growth in crowds, revenue levels and the great interest in the RUGBY WORLD CUP, where will it be in five years' time?

Let us gather more loud voices around us to push the case for skills development, positivity and elegance, as opposed to all might, size and muscle.

There is a balance here and we need to strike it. Parents will demand it or they will vote with their feet, removing their offspring from the colosseum. Spectators will demand it, otherwise they will die of boredom. The players themselves will demand it, to ensure that not only can they continue playing well into their thirties, but also that once they've finished playing that they are not half-crippled. The mentality is going in the wrong direction and it needs to change. World Rugby as a body will not do it unless there is a strong groundswell of opinion making the case for this change.

As players get bigger and bigger, do we still need fifteen players? Is the future of pitches going to be synthetic, AstroTurf material or will something better be invented in time to come? Will players be forced by their own health and protection concerns to wear more body armour or helmets, God forbid!

Yes. There are signs that some teams are embracing the need to open up the game. The number of points scored in the opening matches of the season (2018/2019) has been very encouraging.

However, multiple collisions as a thought through tactic can only be accepted as employed by teachers and coaches bereft of a sense of responsibility towards the game's future or possessing minimal creative instinct. Either way, they shouldn't be coaching any age group or standard.

If this high incidence of impact prevails then we can add a fifth 'C' to Chapter Ten, namely that of repetitive concussion – not an exaggeration, but a reality.

International players are categorically informing us that it is not changes to the game or the laws of the game or indeed more rigorous adjudicating that is required. No, they are simply demanding that there should be less games in a season that they are prepared to play. The 'Global Season' has been discussed for three years now, with no changes being made. All we see is a tightening of the various fiefdoms by those who own them, and we hear them stating, 'it's really difficult!' Really? Can owners and senior managers in the various unions around the world continue to gamble with their most precious commodity, the players, in this way? This is akin to farmers growing crops regardless of need and without rotation. People, you are protecting the wrong thing. It's not about protecting the income stream for this year; it's about protecting the players, so that there will be an income stream, year after year.

And let us never forget the values that rugby union espouses, such as:
- The unity of Irish rugby throughout the thirty years of The Troubles and the bond among nations demonstrated by the bravery of the English team players at Lansdowne Road in 1973.
- The significance of the British and the Irish Lions tours, way beyond the realms of rugby; alas are now being jeopardised by a proposed significantly shorter tour.
- The recent opening of the Saracens High School in one of the most deprived areas in London.

We sincerely hope that the game will indeed continue to grow, while at the same time, remaining true to its heritage, without becoming a dinosaur. We hope to see a greater and an enhanced interest from better-informed spectators and players alike, which will require more referees and (sympathetic) legislators.

Of course, the game needs to evolve, just as our lives and our world evolves. Together we all will have to contribute and answer the yet to be formatted questions.

The New Zealand rugby mantra would do well to be adopted by us all:

'Tell me and I will forget,
Show me and I will remember,
Involve me and I will understand'

MOTIVATION and **INSPIRATION** makes up the live, beating heart of the SIMMERGY Ltd.'s proposition. SIMMERGY Ltd. inspires people to get progress planned, commenced, enabled and completed. This is the message that we've set up for the future of rugby union!

We fervently believe that rugby union is the game for all sizes, intellects and talent levels and we implore you, the reader, to join us in 'Lighting the Candle' to express the need for solidarity, so as to fulfil people's enjoyment, way into the future.

It's about persuading the coaches, the players and the legislators to think very hard about today's game and behave accordingly. Winning is important, but so too is the style of winning, as well as clarity on some of the grey areas that have crept into the game in recent times. For all of us, wherever we see bad practice and believe inherently that this should change, we can make noise, we can write letters and articles and, most of all, we can vote with our feet and our wallets!

We all, of course, have a choice and it is our appeal to you, to please join our mission to make the game that we describe, possible.

APPENDIX

ACKNOWLEDGEMENTS

1. Various columns and articles in the Rugby Reporting newspapers and their journalists, notably:
   a. The Sunday Times, Stephen Jones and Stuart Barnes;
   b. The Daily Telegraph, Mick Cleary;
   c. The Rugby Paper, Peter Jackson and Brendan Gallagher.
2. Sky Sports and BT Sport for showing the games that we couldn't get to.
3. Various Bath rugby personnel for great insight.
4. A well renowned international referee who guided us with his insight and his views.
5. Dominic Pike, a schoolmaster who provided us with much insight on the dilemmas and the concerns about rugby in schools.
6. The inspiration of James Kerr's book 'Legacy' about the All Blacks.
7. The Talbot Hotel and the China Town Restaurant in Oundle, Northamptonshire, for giving us somewhere to meet and to chat whilst preparing this book.
8. Mrs Anne Simmonds and Mrs Helen Russell for putting up with two, often, grumpy old men.

IF YOU'VE ENJOYED THIS BOOK (OR INDEED, HATED IT)
OR JUST HAVE SOME COMMENTS TO MAKE, PLEASE SEND YOUR COMMENTS,
YOUR QUESTIONS AND YOUR VIEWS TO THE AUTHOR;
COLIN SIMMONDS AND HIS PRIMARY CONTRIBUTOR; IAIN RUSSELL, *via:*
colin@simmergy.com

The author

Colin Simmonds was born in 1955 in the UK. He
attended Ripon Grammar School and thereafter,
Birmingham University. He was employed by
Associated British Foods plc from 1990 until 2017.
His favourite activities were playing rugby union
and cricket. He also enjoys travelling and reading.
Colin's special skills include business strategy and
marketing. He is an accomplished rugby coach
and businessman. He drove the development and
general affairs of several companies. Latterly, he
has pursued a consulting career at SIMMERGY Ltd;
and while there he mentored and coached many
young business managers.
As a rugby coach, he worked with several teams at
senior and junior levels. His rugby career comprised
playing for Harrogate Rugby Club, Yorkshire and
Bath rugby clubs. He is married with one son.
Lighting the Candle is his first book.

The publisher

*He who stops
getting better
stops being good.*

This is the motto of novum publishing, and our focus
is on finding new manuscripts, publishing them and
offering long-term support to the authors.
Our publishing house was founded in 1997, and since
then it has become THE expert for new authors and
has won numerous awards.

**Our editorial team will peruse each manuscript
within a few weeks free of charge and without
obligation.**

You will find more information about
novum publishing and our books on the internet:

www.novum-publishing.co.uk